Library of
Davidson College
VOID

Societies in Upheaval

Recent Titles in Contributions to the Study of World History

The Myth of the Revolution: Hero Cults and the Institutionalization of the Mexican State, 1920–1940
Ilene V. O'Malley

Accommodation and Resistance: The French Left, Indochina and the Cold War, 1944–1954
Edward Rice-Maximin

Genocide and the Modern Age: Etiology and Case Studies of Mass Death
Isidor Wallimann and Michael N. Dobkowski, editors

Because They Were Jews: A History of Antisemitism
Meyer Weinberg

Societies in Upheaval

INSURRECTIONS IN FRANCE, HUNGARY, AND SPAIN IN THE EARLY EIGHTEENTH CENTURY

Linda Frey and Marsha Frey

CONTRIBUTIONS TO THE STUDY OF WORLD HISTORY, NUMBER 6

GREENWOOD PRESS

NEW YORK
WESTPORT, CONNECTICUT
LONDON

Library of Congress Cataloging-in-Publication Data

Frey, Linda.
   Societies in upheaval.

   (Contributions to the study of world history,
ISSN 0885–9159; no. 6)
   Bibliography: p.
   Includes index.
   1. Spanish Succession, War of, 1701–1714. 2. France—
History—Louis IV—1643–1715. 3. Hungary—History—
1683–1848. 4. Spain—History—Philip V, 1700–1746.
5. Revolutions—Europe—History—18th century. I. Frey,
Marsha. II. Title. III. Series.
D282.F73   1987   940.2′526   86-25744
ISBN 0-313-25592-X (lib. bdg. : alk. paper)

Copyright © 1987 by Linda Frey and Marsha Frey

All rights reserved. No portion of this book may be
reproduced, by any process or technique, without the
express written consent of the publisher.

Library of Congress Catalog Card Number: 86-25744
ISBN: 0-313-25592-X
ISSN: 0885-9159

First published in 1987

Greenwood Press, Inc.
88 Post Road West, Westport, Connecticut 06881

Printed in the United States of America

The paper used in this book complies with the
Permanent Paper Standard issued by the National
Information Standards Organization (Z39.48-1984).

10 9 8 7 6 5 4 3 2 1

To our mother

Contents

	ACKNOWLEDGMENTS	ix
	PREFACE	xi
1.	Theories and Revolutions	1
2.	France	37
3.	Hungary	61
4.	Spain	83
5.	Conclusions	105
	A SELECT BIBLIOGRAPHY OF PRINTED SOURCES	127
	INDEX	139

Acknowledgments

We would like to acknowledge the generous support and encouragement of our colleagues, particularly Peter Sugar, George Kren, and Donald Mrozek, and of our deans, Howard Reinhardt, Robert Kruh, and William Stamey. The American Council of Learned Societies and the United States Office of Education aided us, as did the staff and directors of the Archives des Affaires Étrangères, the Algemeen Rijksarchief, the Bayerisches Hauptstaatsarchiv, the British Museum, the Stadtarchiv Hannover, the Österreichisches Staatsarchiv, Haus- Hof- und Staatsarchiv, the Országos Levéltár, the Public Record Office, Ráday Levéltár, Zentrales Staatsarchiv (Merseburg), the Library of Congress, and the libraries at Kansas State University, the University of Montana, and Indiana University. Without their patience and assistance this work would not have been possible. Many Hungarians, both here and abroad, have supported our research and have opened their archives, their homes, and their hearts to us. Our secretaries, Julie McVay, Betty Bailey, and Nedra Sylvis, helped us immeasurably, as did our mother and our canine crew.

Preface

From the banks of the Tisza to the mountains of the Cévennes to the shores of the Mediterranean, insurrections broke out in the early eighteenth century. The almost simultaneous eruption of insurrections in three widely scattered locations—Hungary, France, and Spain—during the War of the Spanish Succession (1702–1714) prompted us to examine the nature and causes of revolution and the preconceptions and mythology surrounding that term. More specifically, an inquiry that focuses on these crises reveals much about the manifestations of discontent and about the role and limitations of the state in early modern Europe. It was an era in which the discontented could still win concessions from the central government, an era in which alternatives to the existing socioeconomic system were not available and were not envisioned. In all three instances traditions of protest molded the course of the revolt, the agrarian depression and the fiscal pressures set the stage, and autonomous organizations threatened the power of the absolute state. Comparative history, for all its inherent and formidable difficulties, offers the possibility of providing a different perspective on seemingly disparate events in Hungary, France, and Spain. This study underscores the gap between early modern and modern Europe and provides a vehicle for examining the validity of the models and frameworks developed by social scientists. Just as Alice in Wonderland eats the magic mushroom, making herself larger or smaller to fit the circumstances, so social scientists attempt to make history fit their respective theories. Scholars often find themselves in a wonderland where time has stopped, where the tea party goes on and on. Social scientists often ignore the specificity of events and apply models far removed from the reality of early modern Europe. Otto Hintze succinctly pinpointed the differences between a social scientist and a historian. "You can compare in order to find something general that underlies the things that are compared," he wrote, "and you can compare in order to grasp more clearly the singularity of the thing that is compared, and to distinguish it from others. The sociologist does the former; the historian the latter."[1] We will be happy to adopt the role of historian.

NOTES

1. Quoted in Perez Zagorin, *Rebels and Rulers, 1500–1660* (Cambridge, 1982), 1:27.

Societies in Upheaval

1
Theories and Revolutions

At the Diet of Ónod (1707) two of Ferenc Rákóczi's adherents, Counts Miklós Bercsényi and Sándor Károlyi, drew their swords and murdered Meynhért Rakovszky, a nobleman who opposed the continuance of the war; they did so in full view of the assembly. On the Feast of the Holy Innocents (28 December 1705) the Spanish assaulted and murdered the French troops who were passing through the city of Saragossa. In the Cévennes, French peasants, dubbed Camisards, seized a number of pregnant Catholic women and slew them, tearing the fetuses from their wombs (1702). A cold-blooded execution, frenzied mob violence, and ritualistic murder marked the insurrections that shook Europe during the War of the Spanish Succession (1702–1714).

What differentiated this violence from common crime was its motivation. These acts were political crimes. Particularly in the Cévennes the rebels repudiated basic norms and conventions; they engaged in terroristic activities, as did the government. Both sides resorted to "the systematic use of extreme violence and threats of violence in order to achieve public or political objectives."[1] The rebels did not engage in systematic terrorism as Walter Laqueur defines it, because they used terror only as a subordinate strategy.[2] What they shared with modern terrorists was their antinomianism, that is, their conviction that the promotion of their cause exempted them from traditional mores, from humanitarian considerations. They engaged in "subrevolutionary" terrorism, for they protested governmental interference with a way of life; the Camisards resented the destruction of the Huguenot community, the Hungarians and the Aragonese the loss of their traditional liberties. The government, through men such as Sigbert Heister in Hungary and Nicolas Lamoignon de Basville in France, engaged in repressive terrorism aimed at suppressing the insurgents.[3] Even before the revolt in the Cévennes broke out, Basville had advocated terror in the conviction that it would discourage rebellion. In Hungary poorly disciplined Croat and Serb irregulars were notorious for their atrocities. They often roasted their victims alive or stuffed them with gunpowder before igniting them. Such violence was both instrumental, in the sense that it was used as means to another end, and expressive, in that it stemmed from feelings of anger or fear.

The rebels also used violence, such as the castration or execution of Catholic priests in the Cévennes and the slaying of Frenchmen in Aragon, in part to dramatize their grievances. During the latter stages of the Rákóczi war the rebels mounted a campaign of terror in the area along the Erblande; they frequently tortured and murdered innocent civilians, including women and children. Throughout the *kuruc* war the insurgents resorted to intimidation, threatening the population with death or expulsion if they did not join the *kuruc* side. At the Diet of Ónod, when Rakovszky and Kristof Okoliczányi complained of the excesses of Rákóczi's troops, the high taxes, the problems caused by the copper money, and the difficulties inherent in supplying the army, Rákóczi's lieutenant Bercsényi railed against them for their ingratitude and their calumnies and ran his sword through the body of Rakovszky. In the ensuing melee Okoliczányi was struck several times. He was later executed.[4] Through these cold-blooded actions, Rákóczi and his lieutenants hoped to quash any resistance to their policies. Terrorism became a hallmark of all three insurrections.

In Hungary the nobility joined with the serfs from 1703 to 1711 to resist, albeit unsuccessfully, what they viewed as the unconstitutional rule of the Habsburgs. Economic grievances, religious persecution, and resentment of foreign, that is, German, rule touched off the conflagration. Rákóczi, the leader of the insurrection, ultimately failed to merge this local conflict with the ongoing larger conflict in the West, the War of the Spanish Succession. This failure, coupled with the loss of popular support and the insoluble economic problems that confronted the Hungarians, doomed the insurrection.

In Spain large sections of the kingdom of Aragon recognized the Austrian claimant, Archduke Charles, as king of Spain, thereby catapulting the land into civil war. Only Castile unswervingly supported the French claimant, Philip of Anjou. The tradition of separatism, resentment of Castilian dominance, and hatred of the French fueled the revolt, which flared up during the early years of the War of the Spanish Succession but subsequently collapsed when the English and the Austrians, contrary to earlier promises, abandoned their commitments and their allies. Alone, the Aragonese faced the reprisals of the Castilians and the French.

In 1702 the Protestants in the Cévennes revolted against their sovereign, Louis XIV. The guilt of apostasy and the consequences of the deculturation of the Protestant subculture bred desperation. The agrarian depression and the rising taxes levied to meet war needs exacerbated the existing economic crisis. Under such conditions messianism and, ultimately, revolt flourished. The religious frenzy of the rebels and the ruthlessness of the king's forces meant an escalation in the level of violence. The royal troops devastated the countryside, as did the harsh winter, which only abetted the king's cause. The majority of the outmaneuvered rebels surrendered in 1704.

These insurrections were only part of the "long litany of revolt," the long "course of violent opposition to authority."[5] In Hungary, in Spain, and in France the insurrectionists responded violently to repression and to "the intolerable," whether it was the imposition of foreign rule or forced deculturation. They engaged in a "lethal dialogue"; they played a "deadly game" with the forces of authority. Revolt was "a dialogue of the desperate with the determined."[6]

An analysis of these three insurrections in Hungary, Spain, and France in the early eighteenth century reflects the limitations of the basic conceptual frameworks developed by historians and social scientists and raises certain fundamental questions about the nature and causes of revolution. Historians, when they speak of revolution, have used the French Revolution as the litmus test by which to judge other insurrections. The French have taken this logic one step further and have assumed that when one speaks about The Revolution one refers to the revolution of 1789 and no other. To Hannah Arendt the preeminence of the French Revolution is ironic, because that revolution, which "ended in disaster[,] has made world history while the American Revolution so triumphantly successful has remained an event of little more than local importance."[7] If the phenomenon of the French Revolution has dominated historiographical interpretation, the Marxists have introduced yet another distortion.

Marxists have emphasized the discontinuity between economic development and social institutions in triggering revolution. Orthodox socialists have adopted a narrow, rigid interpretation of revolution, contending that only the struggles of the proletariat, not those of the peasant masses, can lead to revolution. This Eurocentric assessment fails not only for early modern Europe but for Third World countries as well.[8] When historians view revolutions through the distorting lenses of the nineteenth and twentieth centuries, they no longer interpret these events as unique phenomena but rather see them as part of an extended historical process. "Such a conscious recovery of historical experience may lead the contemporary to become the prisoner of past revolutions"[9]—and for us, past revolts to become the prisoners of future ones. For some, such as Arendt, revolution is only a modern phenomenon, for it is only since 1789 that "the pathos of novelty," the experience of a new beginning, and the idea of freedom have coincided.[10]

Such theories may be useful in explaining the revolts of the modern era but not those of early modern Europe (1500–1789), for they impose certain anachronistic perceptions not easily discarded. The patterns of the twentieth-century revolutions are indeed fundamentally different from those of their historical forerunners. Certain concepts such as class and class conflict have no meaning when applied to the eighteenth century—or if they do have a meaning it is one not commonly understood—while other issues such as religion, regional autonomy, and xenophobia play a crucial role. Different parameters are at work in the eighteenth century.

What, then, distinguishes early modern European insurrections from modern revolutions? The revolutionary models formulated by the political scientist and the sociologist do little to illumine the nature of revolt in the early eighteenth century, but they can point out certain common relationships and perhaps pose larger questions. Many historians, such as Lawrence Stone, have argued:

> Some of the writings of contemporary social scientists are ingenious feats of verbal juggling in an esoteric language, performed around the totem pole of an abstract model, surrounded as far as the eye can see by the arid wastes of terminological definitions and mathematical formulae.[11]

Typical of these types of constructs is that of Chalmers Johnson, who has delineated six types of revolution: the jacquerie, the millenarian rebellion, the anarchistic or perhaps better styled the nostalgic rebellion (which romantically idealizes the past), the Jacobin-Communist revolution, the conspiratorial coup d'état, and the militarized mass insurrection.[12] These early-eighteenth-century insurrections do not fall within any one of Johnson's six categories.

The Camisard revolt had elements of both the jacquerie and the millenarian revolution. It was a jacquerie in the sense that the rebels had limited aims; they wanted to restore a lost right: the right of liberty of conscience, the right to practice their religion. The rebels sought these changes without challenging either the community (which they sought to defend) or the regime (which they did not explicitly denounce). They voiced the hope that the king would convert, but they never expected the system to change. "Fin du clergé, vive notre bon Roy," they cried. They did not envisage massive structural changes. The leaders did not attempt to overthrow the aristocratic/monarchical structure but to co-opt it. For example, they adopted the titles, such as *comte Roland*,[13] and even the clothing of the nobility. They structured "their world through models provided by the dominant group."[14] Their victims were identifiable by their faith, Catholic, or their vocation, soldier, not by their social class. Catholic peasant women died along with Catholic seigneurs and errant priests. The rebels' goals were consonant with the traditional structure; they sought to reconstitute the old system, not to destroy it.

The revolt also fits the jacquerie model because its leadership came from the peasantry and because it occurred spontaneously, flaring up after the murder of the local abbot and spreading through the various prophets. It became a revolution of the masses. Preconditions such as poverty and religious intolerance existed for a long time, until the pressure of war and the appearance of prophets triggered the insurrection. The Camisard revolt was not a traditional peasant revolt. Contemporaries, however, could judge the revolt only in terms of past revolts. This limited their vision and meant that they emphasized the antifiscal nature of the troubles. The intendant Basville, however, made no reference to complaints about taxes. Nor did the Camisard revolt have the ephemeral character of other popular revolts. The unusual length of their resistance can be attributed only to the desperate energy government repression had unleashed.[15] This was not a war that neatly fit the traditional norms. We do not hear the traditional complaints. In 1637 the Croquants of Perigord lamented: "We have given more than we are able to bear"; "We are unable to meet a thousand new charges that were unknown to our fathers"; "[The financiers have sent] among us a thousand thieves who eat up the flesh of the poor husbandmen to the very bones."[16] Such plaints characterized jacqueries but not the Camisard revolt.

The Camisard revolt also had overtones of a millenarian rebellion, particularly as defined by Norman Cohn. It was part of a long line of movements inspired by religious visions. It occurred in a society in which religion "determine[d] and dominate[d] the total world outlook" and in a period "when the political and religious aspects of society were still largely undifferentiated."[17] Religious ideas permeated the ethos of the Camisard society. When the existing structure of a society (in the case of the Camisards the Huguenot community) is undermined, the members become less able to face calamity. Cohn argued that "revolutionary chiliasm has flourished only where the normal familiar pattern of life has already undergone a disruption so severe as to seem irremediable."[18] The collapse of the traditional value system created a sense of disorientation, frustration, and guilt. The Camisards were haunted by the guilt of apostasy. With the disintegration of the religious community, the Camisards found themselves deprived of the material and emotional support to which they had become accustomed. At the same time, many faced poverty or famine. Such calamities caused by little-understood forces, Cohn argued,

> may then produce an emotional disturbance so widespread and acute, such an overwhelming sense of being exposed, cast out and helpless, that the only way in which it can find effective relief is through an outburst of paranoia, a sudden, collective and fanatical pursuit of the Millennium.[19]

Persecuted minorities, such as the Camisards, who do not have the power to change the social situation or relieve the strain imposed on them typically adopt value-oriented beliefs, such as millenarianism. For the Camisards such beliefs acted as an alternative means to modify the society.[20] The movement answered the search for a sense of community. The government persecution radicalized the movement and enabled the Camisards to interpret their suffering in apocalyptic terms: their sufferings heralded the millennium. The coincidence of persecution with the economic and demographic crises made the Camisards open to a millenarian movement. The stress of deculturation combined with their economic woes created a sense of alienation from life and induced a feeling of escapism. The peasants were vulnerable to millenarian movements because their Judaeo-Christian *Weltanschauung* predisposed them to view history in teleological terms, that is, to imagine that history had an inherent purpose, preordained to be realized on earth at the Second Coming.

This belief galvanized individuals, infusing them with confidence, energy, and, as we will see, ruthlessness. It also isolated them from the reality of the king's power and made them oblivious to ineluctable limitations, assured of their ultimate triumph. The leaders were filled with a spirit of heroic action, a spirit that pitted them against the forces of evil. Their sense of mission imbued the rebellion with an undoubted ruthlessness and brutality. The tale of the revolt echoes a fifteenth-century sect, the Taborites, who preached total chiliastic war. The faithful were enjoined to "plunge the swords into the enemies of Christ and to wash their hands in the victims' blood."[21] The enemies of God were to be exterminated. "The enthusiasm of these groups, the spirit of total dedication to a cause of overriding importance, the conviction of doing God's will, often lead to a dehumanization of the opponent who is conceived as all evil and all depraved."[22]

The religious dimension heightened the intensity of the conflict and enabled the insurgents to create a reality different from that forced on them.[23] The Camisard revolt makes the most sense if interpreted as a collective effort to cope with a situation of strain, dominated by prophetic visions and an apocalyptic mentality. The commitment to a future world led to a certain antinomianism, a rejection of traditional norms best illustrated by the sexual exhibitionism of some of the assemblies. This new morality with its ritualized violation of former taboos strengthened the group's identity, as did mass possession and physical phenomena such as convulsions. Such motor responses provided an outlet for the strain induced by deculturation and physical deprivation. As in other millenarian movements, women played an important role, as did many of the prophets, who became rebel leaders. Although most believed in the coming of the millennium, none envisaged, as do most millenarians, the total transformation of the social system; none postulated eschatological goals. These visionaries did not call for the overthrow of the king or the abolition of social distinctions but instead prophesied the conversion of the king and the reconciliation of the French. Typically, the Camisards displaced their hostility and blamed not the king but the local intendant Basville. Nor was the Camisard revolt a millenarian rebellion in the sense that it was a harbinger of future fundamental changes. Neither the jacquerie nor the millenarian model alone adequately describes the Camisard revolt. Nor does either explain the crisis engendered by deculturation and adjuration of a faith. To contemporaries and to many subsequent historians, the tale of the Camisards remained "une histoire impossible."[24]

The Hungarian insurrection fits the traditional categories even more poorly, for it has elements of a jacquerie, an anarchistic revolution, and a militarized mass insurrection. The rebellion began as a traditional jacquerie. The peasants launched a spontaneous uprising triggered by a crushing financial burden. After assuming leadership, Rákóczi transformed the rebellion by calling on the nobility to join the peasantry. Unlike the participants in a jacquerie, these insurgents aimed to overthrow a dynasty, the

Habsburgs. Like an anarchistic rebellion, the rebels' ideology was based on an idealized view of the Magyar past. Accordingly, they demanded the restoration of such traditional liberties as the right to elect their ruler and the right to resist the king with arms. The nobles were particularly susceptible to such an appeal because the integration of Hungary into the Habsburg *Gesamtstaat* undermined their position. They could not fail to see that their traditional roles were threatened because of that change. They could not but disapprove of the changes that were occurring in their society. They aimed not to destroy the government but merely to replace the dynasty. And yet the model anarchistic rebellion is antinationalist, not nationalist or protonationalist as the Rákóczi revolt so patently was.

That distinction brings in the third category, the militarized mass insurrection, which is normally limited to the twentieth century. Yet the Rákóczi revolt aptly fits that category, for it sought to overthrow the Habsburgs by a calculated strategy, one based on mobilization of the masses. The rebels' successful but essentially guerrilla operations were dependent on popular support. When Rákóczi lost that support his cause was doomed. As in other militarized mass insurrections, the elite used propaganda extensively and operated through the establishment of a rebel infrastructure, a virtually autonomous government, which levied taxes and sent envoys to foreign governments. The Hungarians had created a state of multiple sovereignty in which a part of the population obeyed the alternative authority, not the Habsburg government. Last and most important, Rákóczi's appeal was essentially nationalistic. Yet the model of a militarized mass insurrection is a singularly inadequate one for the eighteenth century because the outcome was dependent ultimately on military victory, not on political attitudes.

The revolts in Spain fit the mold of an anarchistic rebellion more than any other typology. Particularly in Valencia, the peasants and lower classes played a significant role and espoused the traditional antitax program of a peasant revolt. As in a jacquerie, the peasants demanded the retention or reestablishment of their traditional rights. Unlike a jacquerie, these revolts were not led by peasants. The rebels aimed, as in an anarchistic revolution, to overthrow the regime, that of Philip V. In Catalonia the argument is even clearer, for there the peasants did not play as important a role as they had in 1640. The lesser nobility and the bourgeoisie played the crucial roles, basing their goals on an idealized past. That idealization made the disparity between the real and the ideal even more unpalatable. Just as the rebels in 1640 had stressed the importance of a "constitutional system built on the firm foundations of law and representation and on a binding contractual relationship between the prince and his subjects,"[25] so too did those in the early eighteenth century. The insurgents opposed changes in the traditional structure, especially the concentration of power in the central government and the challenge to their *fueros*. The grandees in particular found their traditional roles threatened.

The insurrections in France, Hungary, and Spain tend to fall within, between, and among the various categories. In Johnson's later four-part typology of simple rebellion, ideological rebellion, simple revolution, and total revolution,[26] they fit in the first category rather than the second, essentially because these rebels were not alienated from the "values embedded in the old value structure."[27] The ideology they did espouse served to structure their values, the values of a people trying to restore a traditional and idealized regime. By his definition they were not revolutionaries, because they did not advocate the establishment of a new social order. Such taxonomies are either so broad as to be meaningless or so narrow as to be useless. The differences between these categories are often unclear. Furthermore, historical events often cannot be rigidly compartmentalized. Even more disturbing, such models pose questions based on our knowledge of the nineteenth and twentieth centuries, questions that sometimes obscure the more important issues of early modern Europe.

Seeking to redress the problems these typologies present, Perez Zagorin has posited five types of rebellion, or, in his view, revolution, in early modern Europe: (1) conspiracy and coup; (2) urban rebellion; (3) agrarian rebellion; (4) provincial, regional, and separatist rebellion; and (5) kingdom-wide civil war against monarchies.[28] Following this schema, the insurrections in France and Hungary would fall into the classification of a provincial rebellion or one that originated in the "grievances of subordinate or provincial kingdoms within dynastic unions." In the case of Hungary and Spain, the Habsburg emperor and the Bourbon king respectively "violated the autonomous liberties of the provincial kingdom" with "an increasingly repressive government."[29] In both instances the rebellions were launched against those who were external to the society. Both insurrections also had elements of the fifth category, the kingdom-wide civil war against monarchies. The Rákóczi insurrection included both the elite and the masses; it was fought within a large geographic area rather than confined to a local region; it represented an attempt to limit or reverse the growing power of the centralizing government, the Habsburgs; and it lasted for more than five years. Rákóczi's followers were highly organized and even formed an alternative government, engaged in ideological debate that included plebeian radicalism, and made the rebellion an issue of international politics.[30] The rebellions in Spain also shared some of the characteristics of the revolutionary civil war, notably its long duration, its broad social participation (in Catalonia), its high degree of organization (particularly again in Catalonia, where the rebels established an alternative political order), and its impact on great power rivalries. Although the Camisard rebellion is not easily reduced to a single model, it is closest to that of agrarian rebellion. The insurgents were primarily (but not exclusively) peasants, it was limited to a restricted area, and it built upon existing structures—but of the Protestant rather than the agrarian community. Yet the insurgents in France expressed exclusively religious aims rather than "the grievances and desires of peasant communities."[31] Although this typology describes early modern insurrection better than other schemata, the word *revolution* seems misleading. Robert Forster and Jack Greene, along with Zagorin, have argued that there were revolutions in early modern Europe, but the issue, a tangled one, has generated controversy. Forster and Greene have adopted a very broad definition of *revolution* as

any sharp, sudden change or attempted change in the location of political power which involved either the use or the threat of violence and, if successful, expressed itself in the manifest and perhaps radical transformation of the process of government, the accepted foundations of sovereignty or legitimacy, and the conception of the political and/or social order.[32]

Zagorin also rejects the concept that revolution must entail a major transformation in society or must be progressive. For him a revolution is any attempt by subordinate groups through the use of violence to bring about (1) a change of government or its policy, (2) a change of regime or (3) a change of society, whether this attempt is justified by reference to past conditions or to an as yet unattained future ideal.[33]

In order to accept Zagorin's argument one must enlarge the definition of *revolution* and step outside one's initial preconceptions. Only then can the term be extended to encompass early modern rebellion.

Nonetheless, one can dispute Zagorin's contention that the line between early modern revolt and modern revolution cannot be maintained without "presupposing a historical progression in which rebellion is merely a stage evolving toward revolution as a goal."[34] There are several reasons for maintaining the conventional distinction between revolution and rebellion. First, even to enter into the controversy of what revolution is pushes one into "the malady of begged questions,"[35] for the word *revolution* has become so elastic as to be almost meaningless, as in "a revolutionary new shampoo." Second, and paradoxically, the term *revolution* has been used almost exclusively to refer to modern upheavals with the specter of the French Revolution and its successors bedeviling us. It is a time barrier we cannot cross.

Third, in the early eighteenth century, revolution was not generally associated with political upheaval; revolution did not have the connotation it has today. Then it meant a movement of heavenly bodies or more generally circular motion or even a restoration or a return.[36] *Revolution*, originally an astronomical term, described the natural, preordained, and irresistible movement of the planets across the heavens. Nicholas Copernicus aptly entitled his work on the circular movement of celestial bodies *De revolutionibus orbium coelestium*. The syllable *re* in the word underlines the concept of a return. Following this definition Thomas Hobbes, in describing the English Revolution, could say, "I have seen in this revolution a circular motion."[37] As late as 1789 an exchange, now made famous, illustrates the contemporary view of revolution as an irresistible force. The king, after hearing of the fall of the Bastille, remarked, "It is a revolt." "No Sire," a noble contended, "it is a revolution." This exchange also illustrates that the word *revolution* had begun to lose its original connotation of a return to certain given conditions or possibilities. After 1789, as another French observer noted, it had "lost its original sense."[38]

Finally, it is not the success or failure of these insurrections or even the extent of the disaffection which they exploit or reflect that precludes the use of the word *revolution*. Rather, the insurrections discussed are not revolutions in the accepted sense of the word because they did not change or even seek to change the basic institutional structure. Roland Mousnier has argued that the insurgents could not even envisage revolutionary goals because they were imbued with "the omnipotence of custom" and the habit of "submitting to an immutable world as agriculturists." The belief in a supernatural eternal order and the respect for custom and tradition also prevented the rebels from turning against the social and political order.[39] They did not articulate an ideological alternative to the existing system.

The Camisards, for example, did not envisage the overthrow of the state or of society. They argued that the Protestants' troubles would end with the king's conversion. Only then would the religious wars end. When they spoke of liberty and tolerance they meant a return to the policies embodied in the Edict of Nantes, nothing else. The Huguenot pastor Pierre Jurieu in his evocatively entitled *Lettres pastorales aux fidèles de France qui gémissent sous la captivité de Babylone* recognized absolute power as legitimate, limited only by certain divine and human laws. He did, however, question the policy of intolerance and the legitimacy of the king who adopted such a policy. The other pastors of the exiled Huguenots proved even more timid. An anonymous pamphlet of 1689, *Les Soupirs de la France esclave*, denounced the despotism of Louis XIV but not monarchy as an institution. One Huguenot even argued that once the king had been convinced of the loyalty of the Huguenots he would protect them. Whatever the king decreed must be endured, for the evils that ensued from disobedience were greater than any stemming from the abuse of absolute power.

Even Jurieu initially argued that the Huguenots must support the state and denounced the royal order prohibiting the hanging of the fleur-de-lys in the Protestant churches. He went on to argue that deliverance could be expected only from God. There were, however, two rights that could not be surrendered, "the right of conservation for the sake of the community and that of conscience and religion for the church." Louis's attempts to destroy both the community and the faith negated the people's duty of obedience. The cause of the Cévennes was that of "God, liberty, and peace."[40] Jean Cavalier reinforces this contention in his *Mémoires* when he argues that the principal reasons for taking up arms were "to avoid going to Mass, to escape persecution and to obtain the liberty to serve God as he commands us."[41] The millenarian tinge to the revolt meant that the Camisards expected divine intervention. They had only to watch for signs of the Second Coming. Such an attitude does not make revolutionaries; revolutions cannot be left to God. The Camisards directed their protests only against specific abuses, not against the hierarchical society; they sought only to destroy that which threatened the community. Envisaging no change in either society or the state, they did not sense any contradiction between their protestations of fidelity to the king and their actions. Roland and others could affirm that they had always been faithful subjects of the king.[42] They did not postulate an alternative to the existing system. They did not adopt a revolutionary ideology. What ideology they did have was cast primarily in religious terms, for the only systematic view they had of the world was religious.

The term *ideology* here refers not to what Karl Mannheim defined as established values or those complexes of ideas which reinforce the existing order but rather to what he defined as utopia, that is, an innovative belief system, ideas that shatter the prevailing order of things. The very creation of utopia "poses both a counterimage of the existing order and a critique of its ideologies." After a period of time, this dissent develops into a rational critique of existing society.[43] Ideology for us, then, represents an alternative value structure. The insurgents did not have that ideology or what Antonio Gramsci has called a counterideology, an antidote to the existing ideology that makes the people willing partners in their own subjection. Only this counterideology, Gramsci argued, can destroy the hegemony of the ruling classes, the consensus they have been able to impose.[44] In early modern Europe the insurgents had a basically traditional outlook; they tended to look back, to seek to restore traditional rights, which were perceived as threatened.

This does not deny that even retrospective programs or demands can generate unintended consequences or can even lead to innovation. It could be argued that in the early days of both the French and the American Revolution the actors believed that they were restoring the old order.[45] Thomas Paine carried this logic one step further and labeled them both "counterrevolutions." Theorists throughout the seventeenth and eighteenth centuries defended rebellion as the restoration of former rights and privileges, not the establishment of a new order. For Locke, the violation of basic rights that had existed before the formation of governments provided the rationale for revolt. Although the outlook of early modern man extends beyond protest, it cannot bring man to revolution as it is traditionally defined. To advance to the revolutionary state, Gramsci believed, inherent beliefs had to be mingled with a "derived" ideology that posited drastic reform.[46] Early modern Europe was an epoch that presented, however, "one unambiguously perceivable world order."[47] It did not present an alternative.

If ideology is defined as "a specific set of ideas designed to vindicate or disguise class interest,"[48] we introduce yet another distortion, for early modern Europe was organized not by class but by rigid, exclusive orders. Man before the nineteenth century lived in a society of status, a society where law and custom governed the hierarchy of privileges and obligations and defined the traditional order. The *ancien régime* presupposed the inequality of men. It was a society where wealth generally followed power, not power wealth; it was a highly stratified society, built on social and economic inequality, where status and privilege were not solely determined by the economic production of goods. The stratification of society entailed a hierarchy of wealth, power, and privilege not only between but also within the orders.[49] In early modern Europe classes in the Marxian sense did not exist. To even talk in terms of a class struggle in early modern Europe obscures rather than clarifies the issue.

It was a society without class consciousness, but that does not mean that it was a society without social conflict. These revolts tended to follow the model set forth by Mousnier rather than that of Boris Porshnev. While both models analyze revolts in seventeenth-century France, the latter interprets the revolts in terms of class conflict whereas Mousnier more realistically stresses the alliance of different groups, nobles, townsmen as well as peasants, an alliance forged by the resistance to the state.[50] Yet even Mousnier's analysis with its emphasis on economic causes is not without problems for understanding the Camisard revolt. Michel Foucault's argument that power should be understood as a multiplicity of power relations casts light on this issue. For him there is no unified class that organizes rebellions. "There is a plurality of resistances each a special case, distributed in an irregular way in time and space. Sometimes a broad series of resistances converges to bring about a major upheaval."[51]

The Marxist view that "the whole history of mankind...has been a history of class struggles, contests between exploiting and exploited, ruling and oppressed classes"[52] works even less well than other theories. Generally these revolts divided society not horizontally but vertically.[53] In Hungary, for example, the serfs and the nobles joined together under Rákóczi's leadership to fight the Habsburgs. In Spain, particularly in Catalonia, Charles received the support of some of the grandees and many of the lesser nobility, the middle classes, and the peasants. Only in Valencia did the uprisings in favor of Charles assume the tones of a social insurrection. There the Habsburgs gained the support of the peasants and the lower clergy. In France, although the Camisards were mainly peasants and artisans and very few of either the middle class or the nobility participated, this insurrection too had none of the overtones of a class struggle. The victims were selected essentially because of their religion, not their social class. Certainly there were indications of social tensions. But it was the Catholic adversaries, the *Camisards blancs*, who attacked "rich" Protestant patrons. The Camisard revolt can be understood only in terms of a confrontation between "two radically different cultural universes."[54]

The evidence, then, does not support a narrowly conceived Marxist interpretation. The Camisard rebellion was not part of an ongoing class struggle fought under the guise of religion. It was a war of the elect against the godless. Various Marxist scholars like Ernst Werner have argued that medieval millenarian movements were manifestations of the class struggle. Others like Werner Stark have contended that Marxists are "by and large within their rights when they claim that sect movements are phenomena of an ongoing class struggle in societies within which the class conflict has not yet become conscious." Even non-Marxists like Richard Niebuhr have argued that "apocalypticism has always been most at home among the disinherited. The same combination of need and social experience brings forth in these classes a deeper appreciation of the radical character of the ethics of the gospel."[55] This argument, initially so compelling, slights the dominant dimension of the confict, the religious. Second, it was not the most downtrodden of the population who became involved either in the medieval movements or in the Camisard rebellion. The Camisards were primarily artisans and peasants. They lived well enough to be able to gather and horde provisions. Third, it was not surprising that peasants made up the majority of the insurgents, since they were the majority of the population at large. Fourth, as Norman Cohn has argued, "If poverty, hardships and an often oppressive dependence could by themselves generate it, revolutionary chiliasm would have run strong amongst the peasantry of medieval Europe. In point of fact it was seldom to be found at all."[56] Although the social milieu cannot be ignored, factors other than economic exploitation or social tension are pivotal to the emergence of a millenarian movement.

The popular uprisings in Hungary and in Spain were dependent on securing the allegiance or support of the ruling groups. In Hungary they turned to Rákóczi; in Spain, to the bourgeoisie and to an alienated nobility, who feared the loss of their traditional rights. In such a society the rebels were forced to appeal to those in power, those least likely to alter the aristocratic/monarchical framework of the state. If they could not gain that support or if they lost it, the rebels were forced to look abroad for assistance, revealing, as J. H. Elliott has noted, "something of their character and their limitations."[57]

In all three instances the rebels appealed to outside powers. In Hungary, for example, Rákóczi strove to merge a small localized struggle into an ongoing international one, the War of the Spanish Succession. His ultimate failure meant the collapse of the insurrection. He had tried to gain the support of not only the Habsburgs' enemies, France and Bavaria, but the Habsburgs' allies as well, notably England and the United Provinces. The allies had at least given Rákóczi no false promises as they had the Aragonese. Those revolts, inextricably intertwined with the disputed question of the succession in Spain, had also been dependent on foreign intervention for their success. The allies had sent military forces to aid the insurgents, who were after all fighting for their cause. That aid had not prevented the ultimate betrayal. Both the English and Charles VI, Holy Roman Emperor, had assured the Catalans in particular that they would secure their rights at the general peace. Emboldened by such a promise, the Catalans had fought on desperately even after the allies' withdrawal. Philip V's forces did not take Barcelona until 1714, more than a year after the Treaty of Utrecht was signed. But the imperial and English promises were not kept. The Catalans had continued to fight and Rákóczi to hope. But both were chimeras, as were the Camisards' illusions that they would obtain significant outside assistance from the Protestants and the other allied powers.

The allies could not but view the Camisards as an important diversion in the war against Louis XIV or, as one English representative dubbed them, "the Queen's cheapest allies."[58] Nonetheless, the allies at first hesitated to send aid, in part because of their reluctance to sanction rebellion and in part because of their conviction that the rebels could not seriously check the royal forces. Persuaded by the strength of the Camisard resistance, the allies eventually sent help, but it arrived too late. The allies had dispatched two agents, David Flotard[59] in 1703 and Tobie de Rocayrol in 1704, and, in the summer of 1703, two English frigates that remained off the coast. In 1704 the allied fleet attempted to land men near Aigues-Mortes in the Golfe du Lion but was dispersed by a storm. The French captured one of the *tartanes*, executed the officers, and condemned the others to the galleys. Various other allied plans came to naught. For example, the English and the Dutch had sent money to Geneva that was intended to support the Cévennois.[60] Tobie de Rocayrol betrayed his friends in 1707 when he approached the French with the allied plans to aid the rebels. For his trouble, the French imprisoned him and sentenced him to the galleys at Marseilles. They had already discovered the rebels' plans to coordinate their actions with an allied offensive. An allied force did land on the coastline at Sète in 1709 but withdrew after the French army, again apprised of allied plans, appeared on the scene. Was there yet another agent at the English court? In July 1710 the allies sent a diversionary force with the intention of relieving the pressure on Catalonia by drawing the French troops under the duc de Noailles to the east. The soldiers did embark in Bas Languedoc but were forced to withdraw. The allied intervention had been too little and too late. Once the negotiations for the Peace of Utrecht had begun, the allies neglected the Huguenot cause. In the final treaty, the allies did not insert any provisions that would have protected the Protestant underground in France.[61] The government had triumphed. In spite of the length and ferocity of the rebellion, the Camisards were unable to challenge state power effectively. They could but leave to the Huguenots a legend of resistance. "L'histoire des Camisards," wrote one, "est notre chanson de geste, notre Iliade, notre Odysée et notre légende dorée."[62]

The ultimate failure of the insurrections in the Cévennes, Hungary, and Spain and their dependence on outside aid illustrate the fundamental weakness of rebellion in early modern Europe. The rebels in all three areas had resorted to guerrilla warfare; indeed, they had no choice. They also had limited success. Although between fifteen hundred and two thousand Camisards had held twenty-five thousand soldiers in check, they could not triumph. The guerrillas could never win on their own. In all three instances the power of the government proved overwhelming. Nonetheless, guerrilla warfare was not uncommon in early modern Europe, particularly during the War of the Spanish Succession, as the Castilian harassment of Allied troops and the Tyrolean resistance to the Bavarian army attest. It is sometimes assumed that guerrilla warfare began with the Spanish resistance to Napoleon in the Peninsular Wars. Indeed, the very term *guerrilla* ("little war") comes from Spanish and dates from the nineteenth century. But one can trace guerrilla warfare back to the very beginnings of history. The Bible, for example, recounts the struggle of Judas Maccabeus against the Greco-Syrian conquerors in the first century B.C. The Spanish and the French organized a revolt against the established government just as Spartacus had earlier when he revolted against Rome. The Hungarians, on the other hand, launched an uprising against foreign occupation just as the Scythians had resisted the Persian occupation in 512 B.C.[63]

In all three cases the insurgents employed typical guerrilla tactics such as harassment of the enemy, evasion of pitched battles and frontal confrontations, and launching of surprise attacks. It has been argued that the Rákóczi revolt "constitutes the longest self-sustained guerrilla war in early modern times."[64] Undoubtedly the

Hungarians excelled in light mobile unconventional warfare, but the line between regular and irregular operations is not a firm one. When guerrillas feel strong enough they often turn to conventional tactics, as did Rákóczi. When the Hungarians resorted to conventional warfare they invariably lost, as they did at Trencsén in August 1708. The Spanish inevitably failed when allied support was withdrawn.

In both Aragon, particularly Catalonia, and Hungary, peripheral areas where the hold of the government was tenuous at best, a long tradition of guerrilla warfare existed. Ever since the battle of Mohács in 1526, which resulted in the division of Hungary between the Turks and the Habsburgs, the Hungarians had employed unconventional warfare, using mobile units to pillage the frontier districts. During the Rákóczi war they succeeded in raiding as far as Vienna in the summer of 1704. But thereafter these forays decreased, particularly after the establishment of a permanent fortification system along the Styrian Hungarian border in 1706.[65] When forced to retreat the Hungarians often devastated the surrounding countryside, such as the region around Kassa in 1706, in order to destroy any available provisions for the Austrian army. The mountainous terrain of the Cévennes and parts of Aragon made these regions more inaccessible to government troops and proved ideal for unconventional warfare, as did Eastern Europe, which has been dubbed the classic region for guerrilla warfare. Rákóczi used northeastern Hungary's mountainous regions, where the insurrection had started, as his base. Yet another requisite of successful guerrilla operations was the support of the population. Once Rákóczi, for example, lost mass support his cause was doomed.[66]

Although these conflicts can be understood in the larger context of guerrilla warfare, most of the models or theories developed to explain revolutions do not fit the revolts of the early eighteenth century. The discrepancy between the models and the revolts highlights the problem of classifying these insurrections as revolutions and the additional problem of applying models so distant from the reality of the eighteenth century. The structural-functional analysts, for example, presuppose a "functionally integrated social system," a social order in a state of "homeostatic equilibrium." When forces of change, whether outside or inside, impinge on the system, either it will find a new equilibrium, or the pressures will produce "dissynchronization" or "system disequilibrium." If the social order cannot adapt or adjust to change, the society will be in a state of dysfunction. At this point, if the leaders do not act to restore equilibrium because of intransigence or incompetence, this state of multiple dysfunction will lead to disaffection, creating the potential for revolution. One event, such as the execution of Françoise Brès in the Cévennes, can act as a trigger or an accelerator, can then bring on revolution.[67] The problem is that such accelerators do not always and need not automatically trigger a revolution, which is thus viewed as a violent response to dysfunction. As has been often pointed out, the structural-functional analysts extend the concept of equilibrium so far that it becomes "coterminous with that of organized society; what then is actually discussed is not so much a set of equilibrium conditions as a set of minimum conditions of social existence."[68] A functioning system is by definition in a state of equilibrium. If the functionalist equilibrium model can be applied to any society, which is doubtful, it certainly cannot be applied with any seriousness to the turbulence of early modern Europe, a society where violence was endemic, "a volcano with many craters."[69] This system would by definition be in a state of "perpetual disequilibrium" or "endemic dysfunction," a condition impossible to redress because of elite intransigence and inefficient government.

Some functionalists have developed an alternative model that can be more easily applied to early modern European society. In this model "all societies are in a condition of multiple and perpetual tension held in check by social norms, ideological beliefs, and state sanctions."[70] In all three revolts the societies could not adjust to either internal or external change. In Spain the rise of the state, the concentration of more and more power in the central government, the abrogation of the traditional *fueros*, and the reduction of the power of the grandees in the political arena challenged established elites, such as the great landed aristocracy. These dialectical changes, which ran "counter to the prevailing regime of values, participation, power or property,"[71] disrupted the society. The wide disparities in economic and demographic growth between the different parts of Spain contributed further to the social tension. The rise of the state with the extension of royal jurisdiction was inherently a destabilizing factor, for it challenged the status of an established elite. In France the attempt to eradicate Calvinism endangered even the existence of the local communities. In Hungary the Habsburg conquest challenged the power and economic base of the old nobility. The extension of the *Gesamtstaat* in Spain, as in France and Hungary, had already disrupted the equilibrium. The pressures of war triggered revolt.

Even if the theory of equilibrium is accepted, the structuralist cannot explain how a given set of conditions can trigger different results at different times.[72] The structural hypothesis, with its emphasis on objective conditions such as prices, mobility, and demography, cannot link conditions and actions. Men do not simply react to changing conditions; within the constraints of certain conditions they can and do make choices, as Charles Tilly has argued.[73] The structuralist paradigm also undervalues the role of the state in shaping institutional structures.[74] The behavioral hypothesis, on the contrary, emphasizes how attitudes are formed, how social conditions are perceived and acted upon, how individuals become revolutionaries. It attempts to explain why conditions formerly viewed as tolerable are later perceived as intolerable. Herein lies the problem: judging how and why perceptions change. Historians of the early eighteenth century do not have the data, especially from the illiterate masses that behaviorists use today. Psychologists emphasize micro data, focusing on the individual, while structuralists emphasize macro data, focusing on the system as a whole. An integration of the two models, macro and micro, can explain why individuals once integrated into a society become alienated and how that alienation stems from dysfunctions in the system. A historical study of revolt in the early eighteenth century can encompass both analyses of objective conditions and inferences regarding subjective reactions to those conditions.

James C. Davies addresses the latter point in his J curve theory; he posits that revolutions are likely to occur when a prolonged period of economic growth is followed by a short period of sharp reversal. The discrepancy between the new expectations and the possibility of their realization creates the potential for revolution. "The actual state of socio-economic development is less significant," according to Davies, "than the expectation that past progress, now blocked, can and must continue in the future."[75] The revolts in Spain best fit this schema. In Spain, parts of Aragon had recovered economically and demographically, possibly as early as if not earlier than the 1670s. Inflationary pressures had lessened, and agricultural prices rose, as did land rents. Economic reversal had not yet occurred, but many feared that it would because of both Castilian and French economic policies. This fear undoubtedly helped to cause the revolt. One could hardly argue that Hungary had undergone a period of sharp reversal, but conditions had continued to deteriorate in many respects under Habsburg rule. The government collected old taxes and levied new ones. It established tariffs and adopted economic policies that disrupted trade patterns and caused an increase in prices even in basic commodities that affected all classes but especially the peasantry. As in France, many abandoned their holdings. Both France and Hungary were devastated lands facing severe labor shortages.

The J curve applies best perhaps to France but only if it can be stretched over a longer period of time and over the generational life of most men of the day. The economic growth that had begun in the Renaissance ended during the reign of Louis XIV. The structural problems of the agricultural economy, compounded by the vagaries of climate and the misguided policies of the central government, triggered the collapse of the rural economy. Even in such circumstances, it would be difficult to argue that the French peasant had Davies' revolutionary mentality, a state of mind that "requires the continued, even habitual but dynamic expectation of greater opportunity to satisfy basic needs."[76] Indeed, as Davies argued, the French peasant's preoccupation with physical survival militated against the establishment of a revolutionary state of mind.

The J curve can of course be applied to developments outside the economic sphere. In many ways the Catalans had enjoyed the luxury of rising expectations. Charles II had ennobled many Catalans and had recognized many of the traditional *fueros*; provincialism and particularism had triumphed in the late seventeenth century. Justifiably, the Catalans, indeed the Aragonese in general, feared the absolutist centralizing policies of Philip V. In Hungary the serfs, who feared losing their independence, had hardly enjoyed a cycle of rising expectations, nor had the nobility, who had seen their privileges being destroyed by an absolute state. Yet the Catalans faced a political reversal; they feared that "ground gained over a long period of time [would] be quickly lost."[77] For the Camisards, in the words of a French observer, "the remembrance of evils past" and the "fear of worse to come" made their "sense of the present insupportable."[78] Since the 1660s the Huguenots had engaged in a kind of desperate royalism designed to assure the king of the loyalty of his Protestant subjects. Yet after 1685 they too faced a loss of rights formerly enjoyed. This loss combined with the guilt of apostasy made them vulnerable to millenarian movements.

Psychological reactions to economic and political change cannot be underestimated. Barrington Moore argues, for example, that it is not the scarcity of resources, not suffering or deprivation, that causes insurrections but the perception of injustice. As Hannah Arendt pointed out, not only injustice but also hypocrisy transforms *engagés* into *enragés*. If the conviction persists that conditions could be changed and are not, rage results.[79] Certain societies can completely adopt an ethic of submission, can learn to accept without question the authority of the oppressor no matter how repressive. Through certain social and psychological mechanisms one can teach and be taught to accept suffering, degradation, and pain as morally justified. In France some undoubtedly viewed their suffering as justified, a punishment from on high for the apostasy of their fathers. Characteristically, the Camisards initially persisted in their belief that the king was a benevolent figure who had only to learn about social injustice in order to correct it.

But insurrection ultimately flared up in France, Spain, and Hungary because the ruler violated the bond of reciprocity, the very cement of the society, by harming individuals without benefiting society as a whole. He violated rules or basic norms accepted by his subjects. One historian has even argued that "the modern idea that all state power requires legitimation by the subjects derives in part from the theories of resistance against governmental or feudal violation of traditional rights developed among the peasant movements of early modern Europe."[80] In Spain, for example, Philip illegally levied taxes to support Castilian troops; in Hungary Leopold violated the oath that he had taken as king and persecuted the Protestants. In both instances the king failed to adhere to his obligations, to keep faith with his subjects. Once the "prevailing system of beliefs that conferred legitimacy" was undermined, the insurrectionists could actively challenge the power of the state, could create effective political organizations that countered its authority. In Spain the rebels could recognize Charles rather than Philip as king; in Hungary they could rally around Ferenc Rákóczi.

For a revolt to break out, suffering and desperation must be combined with moral courage, that is, the capacity to withstand social pressure and resist oppression, and the recognition that certain rules are in fact oppressive. There must also be social support from one's peers. Very rarely is there lone resistance to authority. The "revolutionary personality," according to the Freudians, must have (1) basic trust or self-confidence, a strong sense of security in himself and his social surroundings, (2) self-discipline, a willingness to defer present gratification in the pursuit of long-range goals, and (3) a well-developed conscience that recognizes existing inequities.[81]

Both Rákóczi and Cavalier possessed these traits. Rákóczi both recognized and condemned Leopold's oppressive acts. He willingly sacrificed his wealth and position in order to secure basic Hungarian liberties. In Spain, France, and Hungary militants or activists challenged the dominant mythology; they undermined the "illusion of inevitability". They articulated grievances and urged others to join them—in Hungary, Esze, Bercsényi, and Rákóczi; in Spain, García de Ávila and Bautista y Ramos; and in France, Cavalier, Elie Marion, and Roland. The cultures of all three societies sanctioned the kind of leader-follower relations so integral to charismatic leadership. These leaders motivated their followers by giving them hope—a hope for religious freedom in France, a hope for protection of basic liberties in Spain and in Hungary.

In France the leaders galvanized the masses, mobilizing them in a desperate struggle against the godless. The spread of the revolt was partially dependent on the belief that human action could bring about a millennium and on the charisma of the prophets, who, with a supernatural mandate, helped to legitimize the attack on the existing order. Some of the prophets, such as Abraham Mazel, were not particularly significant individuals. But the rebellions brought into prominence others, such as Roland and Cavalier, who were remarkable individuals, able to elicit devotion and self-sacrifice from those who followed them. Both Roland and Cavalier were charismatic leaders and men of unusual talent. A number of their victories and narrow escapes made them legends in their own time. Imbued with an unwavering faith in his cause, Roland exhibited coolness and remarkable courage when faced with the enemy. The surrender of Cavalier and the death of Roland helped to end the rebellion. The Camisard leaders were typical millenarian prophets in that an episode in each of their lives inspired them to launch a crusade. Their personal religious experiences coincided with the trauma of a people and helped to channel their dissatisfactions.

Rákóczi too was a charismatic leader who had an unshakable faith in the Hungarian cause and was ready to sacrifice everything for it—as he eventually did. His refusal to compromise his beliefs, his refusal to accept the final settlement, meant that he forfeited his patrimony and died in exile from the land he loved. Rákóczi's charisma has persisted throughout the generations. His failure and death could not destroy the Hungarians' faith in him. After his death in 1735 groups of peasants, journeymen, and deserters swore by his name and talked of rising against the emperor. The Hungarian Diet responded by branding him a traitor to king and country and threatening death or torture to those who invoked his name or spread word of his return.[82] Nonetheless, his name continued to circulate, as did rumors of his return. Even today Hungarians revere him as a national hero. His appeal has persisted because he linked himself with the heroes and traditions of the past, articulated widespread grievances, and offered hope to an exploited nation.

Whether in Hungary, in France, or in Spain, "social and cultural space" existed within the prevailing order. A protected enclave, such as the family in the Cévennes, gave the oppressed the opportunity to develop basic traditions and alternative explanations of their social milieu. In France intermittent persecution only succeeded in creating martyrs such as Françoise Brès, not in extinguishing the movement. Brès and others refused to accept their suffering as either legitimate or inevitable. A moral surge of anger or outrage destroyed the sense of legitimacy, the illusion of inevitability, and the dependence upon authority so prevalent in the hierarchical society of early modern Europe. When these perceptions became widely shared and different groups united, revolt broke out. In Hungary both peasants and nobles banded together;

in Spain nobles, bourgeoisie, and lower classes denied Philip's authority.

Once a revolt has begun, the group must redefine itself in relation to its friends and enemies. One of the most effective enemies, because it was one of the most visible, was the foreigner, whether the German in Hungary, the Frenchman or Castilian in Spain, or the outsider in the Cévennes. The foreigner not only is easily identifiable but presents a relatively safe target, for an attack on him does not have all the dangers and implications of an attack on a local power holder. Such visible targets enable the rebels to attract diverse social support while at the same time concealing the divisions and the weaknesses within the group. Once these groups are formed they often resort to violence, repudiating accepted social norms in order to intimidate others into supporting them. Bercsényi's cold-blooded murder of the opposition at Ónod exemplifies this tactic. Rákóczi and others resorted to such tactics only after they had revolted, after they had denied the legitimacy of the existing authority.

Yet another theory, that of relative deprivation as formulated by Ted Gurr, posits that men rebel when they perceive a discrepancy between what they expect and what they are likely to receive.[83] Expectations may rise faster than capabilities, or expectations may remain the same and capabilities may decline. In both instances the deterioration of conditions creates a discrepancy between expectations and the ability to satisfy them. In either scenario the result is anger and discontent. This theory poses a number of problems. First, it is difficult to measure this perceived deprivation; it can only be deduced. Second, in a society filled with tensions, what causes discontent to flare up into rebellion? It is true that in all three insurrections, men generally feared losing what they had gained: local liberties in Spain, noble privileges and free tenure in Hungary, freedom of religion in France. A subjective awareness of distress proved essential in all three rebellions. The relentless fiscal pressures of these societies at war directly threatened men's economic status, as did the growth of the absolute state. Those threats helped lead to insurrection.

Insurrection would not, of course, have been possible no matter how great the discontent without an organized group with certain resources at their disposal. Charles Tilly, refuting the Durkheimian interpretation of a Ted Gurr or a Chalmers Johnson, emphasized the importance of organization rather than social disintegration in triggering collective action.[84] "The motors of militancy are set in motion not by the marginal, the unintegrated and the recently arrived," according to Tilly, "but by [those] who belong to firmly established networks of long standing."[85] In a similar vein, Lynn Hunt has stressed the importance of "networks of family, neighborhood, profession, and social and political associations," which enabled the discontented to act together.[86] Without such resources even widespread discontent would not have triggered revolution. Hunt has also pointed out the invidious connotation of words like *peripheral*, *marginal*, and *outsider*, which seem to imply "isolation, strangeness, extremes" and which are particularly associated "with psychological interpretations of political behavior."[87] Historians have applied just such types of explanation explicitly to the Camisard revolt. Witness the crisis-of-identity or sexual-frustration theories of a Le Roy Ladurie. Yet the men who began the revolts in France, Hungary, and Spain were stable and well-integrated members of the community. These men needed not only group support but also an opportunity, which the War of the Spanish Succession provided. As Theda Skocpol has argued, regimes continue to exist when the masses are disaffected and even when the resources might be available. Only a political-military crisis can create the possibility of revolt.[88]

The nature and scope of the ensuing insurrections reveal much about early modern European society. These revolts should not be construed as demonstrably separate or different from earlier insurrections. In both instances the cohesion of the community, the idealization of the past, and the opposition to the growth of the absolute state consistently recurred. A study of these insurrections can provide insights into the so-called crisis of the seventeenth century. Perez Zagorin has emphasized that for the sixteenth and seventeenth centuries state building and the attendant conflicts contributed "directly or indirectly to the preconditions from which the different revolutions of the time arose."[89] Tilly would agree. For him the processes involved in creating a centralized state explain the essentially defensive nature of collective action and the role of war in triggering such action.[90] Others have stressed that the unprecedented cost of the absolute state's wars coupled with the general economic decline of Europe helped to trigger these outbreaks. Orest Subtelny, for one, hypothesized that "to an even greater extent than in the West, state building and societal reactions to it were the cause of widespread confrontation and conflict in the East." For him the prime cause of the general crisis in both Eastern and Western Europe "was the transition from the noble-association form of government to that of the state-organization." The general time lag between Eastern and Western Europe meant that the general crisis that affected Western Europe in the 1660s affected Eastern Europe about fifty years later, at the end of the seventeenth and the beginning of the eighteenth century. In the early eighteenth century, insurrections in Moldavia, the Ukraine, Livonia, Poland, and Hungary erupted during a major war—the first four during the Great Northern War (1700–1721), the last during the War of the Spanish Succession (1702–1714). In Hungary the Rákóczi war was triggered when the Habsburgs imposed the staggering cost of warfare on a devastated and depopulated land.[91] The xenophobia of the nobles played a key role in that conflict because of the identification of the encroaching Habsburg state with foreign rule. If we accept the time lag theory for the Rákóczi insurrection, were the other insurrections in Spain and France merely echoes, aftertremors of the midcentury earthquake? Was the *ancien régime* as a system now "triumphant and secure"?[92] In France, if rebellion was not eliminated, the nature of the challenge and the challengers had changed. The state had destroyed various autonomous power bases within the land and ensnared the powerful within the system. Nobles participated progressively less and less in rebellion. For Tilly, the "seventeenth century died in a sense, with the demise of the Camisard rebellion." Thereafter, "whole populations of commoners," who had risen "at the sign of the government's violation of its contract with the people . . . rose no more."[93]

These insurrections tell us something not only about this crisis but also about the challenge to the state's authority. The state, as Hegel declared, "stands on earth, and so in the sphere of caprice, chance and error."[94] And error it was. The state in all three instances triggered the insurrections by levying additional taxes, attacking religious liberties, and/or revoking traditional privileges.

The violence followed (it did not precede) a major shift in power in favor of the state. Tilly for one would see these revolts, then, not as abnormal phenomena but as manifestations of a struggle for power.[95] An examination of these three insurrections illumines the power struggles endemic in early modern Europe, the abilities of the monarchic state to implement its policies, and the reactions of ordinary people to the encroachment of the state.

But the models of revolt and revolution postulated by social scientists tell us little about the nature of insurrection in the early eighteenth century, for they ignore the specificity of historical events. The historian embarking on such grounds risks "sacrificing historical specificity for an internally consistent model by which everything and hence nothing can be explained."[96] Social scientists usually base their theories on the French Revolution and thus impose at the outset certain anachronistic perceptions upon the past. They attempt to rigidly compartmentalize historical events, to force them into an ill-fitting Procrustean bed. The insurrections of the early eighteenth century demonstrate the need to revise these constructs. An assessment of the three revolts that broke out during the War of the Spanish Succession will provide a framework for analyzing these issues.

NOTES

1. W. T. Mallison and S. V. Mallison, "The Concept of Public Purpose Terror in International Law: Doctrines and Sanctions to Reduce the Destruction of Human and Material Values," in *International Terrorism and Political Crimes*, edited by M. Cherif Bassiouni (Springfield, Ill., 1975), p. 67.

2. Walter Laqueur, *Terrorism* (Boston, 1977).

3. See Paul Wilkinson, *Political Terrorism* (London, 1974).

4. Ferenc II Rákóczi, *Mémoires du Prince François II Rákóczi sur la guerre de Hongrie depuis 1703 jusqu'á sa fin* (Budapest, 1978), pp. 158–161.

5. J. Bowyer Bell, *On Revolt: Strategies of National Liberation* (Cambridge, Mass., 1976), p. 3.

6. Ibid., pp. 237, 18, 8.

7. Hannah Arendt, *On Revolution* (New York, 1963), p. 49.

8. János Bak and Gerhard Benecke, eds., *Religion and Rural Revolt* (Manchester, 1984), p. 10.

9. Sigmund Neumann, "The International Civil War," in *Why Revolution? Theories and Analyses*, edited by Robert Blackey and Clifford T. Paynton (Cambridge, Mass., 1971), p. 114.
10. Arendt, *On Revolution*, pp. 21–22, 27–28.
11. Lawrence Stone, "Theories of Revolution," *World Politics* 18 (1966):175.
12. Chalmers Johnson, *Revolution and the Social System* (Stanford, Calif., 1964), p. 27 ff.
13. Laporte began a letter, "Nous, Comte et Seigneur Roland, generallissime des protestants de France." The expansion of this salutation into a legend that the revolt was led by a member of the nobility helped contemporaries understand the Camisards' success by reducing it to a model known to them. Philippe Joutard, *La Légende des Camisards: Une sensibilité au passé* (Paris: Gallimard, 1977), p. 81. Joutard presents a fascinating analysis of the French historiographical interpretations on the Camisard revolt.
14. Peter Burke, *Popular Culture in Early Modern Europe* (New York, 1978), p. 173.
15. Joutard, *La Légende*, p. 41.
16. Quoted in Roland Mousnier, *Peasant Uprisings in Seventeenth-Century France* (New York, 1970), pp. 79–80.
17. Guenther Lewy, *Religion and Revolution* (New York, 1974), p. 251.
18. Norman Cohn, *The Pursuit of the Millennium* (London, 1957), p. 310.
19. Ibid., p. 314.
20. Neil J. Smelser, "Structural Conduciveness," in *The Sociology of Revolution*, edited by Ronald Ye-lin Cheng (Chicago, 1973), pp. 21–22.
21. Lewy, *Religion and Revolution*, p. 109.
22. Ibid., p. 243.
23. Harvey Mitchell, Preface in *Rural Revolt*, p. 73.
24. Joutard, *La Légende*, chap. 1. This same historian describes it as a "popular riot, a mystical revolt, a subversive war." Philippe Joutard, ed. *Journaux Camisards (1700–1715)* (Paris, 1965), p. 8.
25. J. H. Elliott, "Revolts in the Spanish Monarchy," in *Preconditions of Revolution in Early Modern Europe*, edited by Robert Forster and Jack Greene (Baltimore, 1970), p. 114.
26. Chalmers Johnson, *Revolutionary Change* (Stanford, Calif., 1982), chap. 6.
27. Johnson, *Revolutionary Change*, p. 123.
28. Perez Zagorin, *Rebels and Rulers, 1500–1660*, 1:41.
29. Ibid., 2:32.

30. Ibid., 2:53, and Orest Subtelny, *Domination of Eastern Europe: Native Nobilities and Foreign Absolutism, 1500–1715* (Montreal, 1986), p. 159.

31. Zagorin, *Rebels and Rulers*, 1:182.

32. See *Preconditions of Revolution* (Baltimore, 1970); A. Lloyd Moote, "The Preconditions of Revolution in Early Modern Europe: Did They Really Exist?" *Canadian Journal of History* 7 (December 1972):207–234; and J. H. Elliott, "Revolution and Continuity in Early Modern Europe," *Past and Present* 42 (February 1969):35–56.

33. Zagorin, *Rebels and Rulers*, 1:17.

34. Ibid., p. 24.

35. Johnson, *Revolution and the Social System*, p. 1.

36. Karl Griewank, *Die neuzeitliche Revolutionsbegriff* (Weimar, 1955).

37. Reinhart Koselleck, *Futures Past: On the Semantics of Historical Time* (Cambridge, 1985), p. 42.

38. Ibid., p. 46.

39. Mousnier, *Peasant Uprisings*, pp. 342–348.

40. Guy H. Dodge, *The Political Theory of the Huguenots of the Dispersion with Special Reference to the Thought and Influence of Pierre Jurieu* (New York, 1947), p. 111 and p. 164.

41. Jean Cavalier, *Mémoires sur la guerre des Camisards* (Paris, 1973), p. 101.

42. Philippe Joutard, "Les Camisards: 'Prophètes de la grande Révolution ou derniers combattants des guerres de religion' " in *L'Ésprit républicain: Colloque d'Orléans 4 et 5 September 1970*, edited by Jacques Viard (Paris, 1972), pp. 113–123.

43. Karl Mannheim, *Ideology and Utopia: An Introduction to the Sociology of Knowledge* (New York, 1936), *Essays on the Sociology of Culture* (London, 1956), p. 146.

44. Quintin Hoare and Geoffrey N. Smith, eds. and trans., *Selections from the Prison Notebooks of Antonio Gramsci*, (London, 1971), pp. 375–377.

45. Alexis de Tocqueville, *The Ancien Régime and the French Revolution* (New York, 1955); and Arendt, *On Revolution*, pp. 37–39.

46. Quoted in George Rudé, *Ideology and Popular Protest* (New York, 1980), pp. 23–35.

47. Mannheim, *Ideology and Utopia*, p. 12.

48. A. Gerschenkron, as quoted in J. H. Elliott, "Revolution and Continuity," p. 42.

49. Jerome Blum, *The End of the Old Order in Rural Europe* (Princeton, N.J., 1978).

50. Boris Fedorovich Porshnev, *Les Soulèvements populaires en France de 1623 à 1648* (Paris, 1963); and Mousnier, *Peasant Uprisings*.

51. Alan Sheridan, *Michel Foucault: The Will to Truth* (London, 1980), p. 185.
52. Karl Marx and Friedrich Engels, *Manifesto of the Communist Party* (New York, 1932), p. 6.
53. René Pillorget, *Les Mouvements insurrectionels de Provence* (Paris, 1975).
54. Joutard, *La Légende*, p. 39.
55. Quoted in Lewy, *Religion and Revolution*, p. 105.
56. Cohn, *The Pursuit of the Millennium*, p. 24.
57. Elliott, "Revolution and Continuity," p. 55.
58. Peter Jones, "Antoine de Guiscard, 'Abbé de la Bourlie,' 'Marquis de Guiscard,' " *British Library Journal* 8 (Spring 1982):100. There are many letters in the recently acquired Blenheim papers, British Museum, Additional Manuscripts, 61257, which includes those of Guiscard and his associates, and 61258, which includes letters from the Camisard leaders and assorted agents; hereafter cited as B.M., Add. Mss.
59. See B.M., Add. Mss. 61258, fols. 85–116, but especially fols. 109–110, the memoir of 1709 of Flotard to the Treasurer, Add. Mss. 61413, fols. 37–38; 61148, fols. 105–108; and 61143, fols. 71–74.
60. B.M., Add. Mss. 38498, fols. 55–58, Townshend to Boyle, 6 and 9 August 1709. Also see B.M., Egerton Mss. 892, Marlborough and Townshend to Boyle, 31 May 1709, fols. 8–10 and Add. Mss. 61169 fols. 54–59, Extracts from the Resolutions of the States General, 28 August 1705.
61. Jones, "Guiscard," p. 111, and *Histoire des Camisards* (London, 1754), 2:370.
62. André Chamson, quoted in Joutard, *La Légende*, p. 281. See Joutard for a discussion of the "legende dorée contre légende noire," two irreconcilable histories, chap. 8.
63. Richard L. Clutterbuck, *Guerrillas and Terrorists* (Athens, Ga., 1977).
64. Charles Ingrao, "Guerrilla Warfare in Early Modern Europe: The *Kuruc* War (1703–1711)," in *Special Topics and Generalizations in the Eighteenth and Nineteenth Centuries*, edited by Béla Király and Gunther E. Rothenberg (New York, 1979), p. 48.
65. Peter Broucek, "The Border Defenses of Lower Austria, Styria and Moravia against the Turks and Rákóczi's Insurgents," in *From Hunyadi to Rákóczi: War and Society in Late Medieval and Early Modern Hungary*, edited by János M. Bak and Béla K. Király, (New York, 1982), pp. 493–513.
66. See Walter Laqueur, *Guerrilla: A Historical and Critical Study* (Boston, 1976); and Lewis A. Gann, *Guerrillas in History* (Stanford, Calif., 1977), for general studies of guerrilla warfare.

67. For a classic exposition of structuralism, see Johnson, *Revolutionary Change*.
68. Alexander Gerschenkron, cited in Zagorin, *Rebels and Rulers*, 1:50. Also see the critique by Anthony D. Smith, *The Concept of Social Change: A Critique of the Functionalist Theory of Social Change* (London, 1973).
69. R. Mandrou, quoted in Zagorin, *Rebels and Rulers*, 1:65.
70. Lawrence Stone, "Theories of Revolution," *World Politics* 18 (January 1966):161.
71. Stephen Haliczer, *The Communeros of Castile: The Forging of a Revolution, 1475–1521* (Madison, Wis. 1981), p. 234.
72. Harry Eckstein, "On the Etiology of Internal War," *History and Theory* 4 (1965):150.
73. Charles Tilly, *From Mobilization to Revolution* (Reading, Mass., 1978) hereafter cited as Tilly, *From Mobilization to Revolution*.
74. See introduction by Theda Skocpol in *Bringing the State Back In*, edited by Peter B. Evans, Dietrich Rueschemeyer, and Theda Skocpol (Cambridge, 1985), pp. 3–37.
75. James C. Davies, "Toward a Theory of Revolution," *American Sociological Review* 27 (February 1962):5–19.
76. Ibid., p. 8.
77. Ibid.
78. Marquis de Guiscard, *The Memoirs of Marquis de Guiscard; or, an Account of his Secret Transactions* (London, 1705), p. 5.
79. Hannah Arendt, *On Violence* (New York, 1969), pp. 63–65.
80. Wolfgang J. Mommsen in *Religion, Politics and Social Protest: Three Studies in Early Modern Germany*, edited by Kaspar von Greyerz (London, 1985), p. xii.
81. Barrington Moore discusses this view in his *Injustice: The Social Bases of Obedience and Revolt* (White Plains, N.Y., 1978), p. 109.
82. Ágnes Várkonyi, "Rákóczi's War of Independence and the Peasantry," in *From Hunyadi to Rákóczi*, pp. 385–386.
83. Ted Gurr, *Why Men Rebel* (Princeton, N.J., 1970), p. 319.
84. See Tilly, *From Mobilization to Revolution*.
85. Tilly and Shorter, quoted by Lynn Hunt, "Charles Tilly's Collective Action," in *Vision and Method in Historical Sociology*, edited by Theda Skocpol (Cambridge, 1984), p. 249.
86. Lynn Hunt, *Politics, Culture and Class in the French Revolution* (Berkeley, Calif., 1984), p. 218.
87. Ibid.
88. Theda Skocpol, *States and Social Revolutions: A Comparative Analysis of France, Russia, and China* (Cambridge, 1979), pp. 16–17.
89. Zagorin, *Rebels and Rulers*, 2:2.

90. Charles Tilly, *The Contentious French* (Cambridge, Mass., 1986), p. 159.

91. Subtelny, *Domination of Eastern Europe*, pp. 110–112.

92. Theodore K. Rabb, *The Struggle for Stability in Early Modern Europe* (New York, 1975), pp. 63–65.

93. Tilly, *The Contentious French*, pp. 46, 160–161, and 178.

94. Quoted by Theda Skocpol, Peter B. Evans, and Dietrich Rueschemeyer, *Bringing the State Back In*, p. 357.

95. Hunt, "Charles Tilly's Collective Action," p. 264.

96. Gary G. Hamilton, "Configurations in History: The Historical Sociology of S. N. Eisenstadt," in *Vision and Method in Historical Sociology*, p. 115.

2

France

The Camisard revolt began with a murder and escalated into a series of atrocities.[1] The murder had been foretold. From the gallows on 16 January 1702 Françoise Brès prophesied the death of the prosecutor, the abbot François de Langlade du Chayla.[2] Du Chayla, the inspector general of the diocese of Mende, had tortured and executed Protestants and made his name a byword for cruelty. The zeal that had earlier served him as a missionary in Siam made him an obvious target in the Cévennes. The religious frenzy that would tinge his murder can be seen in the personality of Abraham Mazel, a visionary and a predicant, or lay preacher. In the early spring of 1702 Mazel dreamed that he drove from the garden a number of fat black steers that were devouring the cabbages. For him the dream was a portent, with the garden representing the church of Christ, Mazel himself the chosen one, and the steers, Catholic priests. So began a crusade against the Catholic church, a "holy war." After joining a band of prophets in the mountains, Mazel was commanded by the Holy Ghost to free his brothers imprisoned at Pont-de-Montvert.[3]

The time for vengeance had come. Directed down to the smallest detail, the prophet, joined now by a group of peasants, walked to Pont-de-Montvert on 24 July 1702, singing psalms. After they demanded that the abbot release the imprisoned Protestants and he refused, they broke down the door and released the prisoners. The condition of their fellow Protestants, who had been tortured and were unable to stand, so infuriated them that they set fire to the house where the abbot had hidden. The speed of the flames that soon engulfed all of the house except the prisons was interpreted as a sign of divine vengeance. Again, the rebels thought, God had intervened, sparing the neighboring homes. The abbot temporarily evaded capture by lowering himself by a rope from a second-story window but broke his leg in the fall. He would have escaped but for the flames, which illuminated the night sky and revealed where he had hidden. Mazel and his companions captured and killed the fleeing abbot. The official autopsy revealed that his body had been pierced fifty-two times and that any one of twenty-four wounds would have been fatal.[4] The hagiographical Catholic perspective is best illustrated by a tract published in 1703, entitled *Relation de la mort de l'abbé Langlade du Chayla et des plusieurs autres personnes qui ont été massacrées par les fanatiques des Cévennes du diocèse de Mende, Toulouse*. In contrast, Mazel argued that the group had carried out "the vengence of heaven," had only slain a "butcher of poor innocents."[5] In his account the Protestants allowed the abbot to say his last prayers and executed him in an orderly fashion. (Here Mazel is obviously seeking to underplay the fanaticism of the rebels.) The group then proceeded to cut off the ears and nose of another priest, Boissonade, and throw him from the church tower and to castrate yet another, who died a few days later. Mazel and his cohorts not only attacked the clergy but also murdered the family of a Catholic seigneur. Fearing further atrocities the curés buried the abbot in haste, wearing civilian garb, and quickly fled to the chateau, protected by soldiers. The intendant voiced his unease: "Voici un temps de tribulations ou il faut veiller."[6] The Cévennes was rapidly becoming an armed camp. One of the prophets was soon caught and condemned to having his hand cut off before being burned alive at Pont-de-Montvert. He died chanting psalms. A portent, a dream, a convulsion, a murder, a castration: thus began what has been called the last war of religion. It has also been known as the *camisard* revolt because the insurgents wore a kind of blouse—*chemise* (in French), *camiso* (in Languedocian)—over their clothes to identify themselves or over their heads to disguise themselves. The word *camisard* might also have originated from *camisade*, meaning night attack.[7]

Historians and even contemporaries who have attempted to understand the Camisards in terms of previous peasant uprisings, to equate peasant insurrection with antifiscal revolts, have dubbed it the last peasant war.[8] Had the fiscal demands of a society at war helped to ignite the rebellion? Taxes on income rose substantially from the War of the League of Augsburg (1688–1697) until the death of the Sun King (1715). From 1690 to 1715 the *taille* rapidly increased not only in nominal value, partly justified by a general rise in prices, but more importantly in real value. An additional burden, the *capitation*, was levied beginning in 1695. Such taxes fell heaviest on landowners, who faced a falling standard of living. The brutal impact of royal taxation can be appreciated if it is realized that under Richelieu and Mazarin taxes had reached what economists view as the natural limit, between 5 and 10 percent of the gross national product. Louis XIV's wars caused an increase of approximately 50 percent in the rate of taxation and threatened to destroy the agrarian economy.[9] In the latter years of Louis XIV's reign the French peasant could have paid ten times as much in taxes as he would have in 1600. Taxes rose markedly from Louis XIV's accession to the end of the seventeenth century and then leveled off.[10] The fiscal charges, especially taxes, combined with existing indebtedness and the burden of usury, only deepened an existing agrarian depression. Contrary to all economic dictates or logic, the government, instead of curtailing its demands, increased them by levying additional taxes on an already impoverished land and on a populace facing a crisis in living standards.

The economic expansion that had begun in the Renaissance came to an abrupt end in the last quarter of the seventeenth century. Land ownership had become polarized as large landowners expanded their lands, forcing out the middling owners and squeezing the rest into miserably small plots.[11] A holding large enough to support a family cost a century's wages for a day laborer.[12] The fragmentation of peasant tenures proved excessive and the tax increases intolerable because production and productivity remained at a level that was centuries old. The cultivators lacked working capital, credit, and livestock. The decimation of the herds by the epizootic diseases of 1676 and 1682 meant less manure and a consequent drop in food production. Profits vanished when the cultivator could not compensate for a decline in prices by an increase in productivity. After 1680 the gross product sank to the level of the sixteenth century or even earlier. But although the gross product fell, the population, costs, and needs had increased. The result was predictable: a violent contraction during the reign of Louis XIV and a partial collapse of the rural economy.

The most crucial impasse to expansion was not monetary but technological. The French peasant persisted in haphazard farming methods: cultivating with wooden implements, exhausting the fields. His inability to increase productivity over the long run meant rural contraction, for the small owner found that the price of grain could not cover his fixed costs. From 1680 to 1690 the peasants continually faced ruin. As production on the exhausted soil declined, land rents fell. The inflexibility of costs combined with the technological weakness of the society meant the end of profitability. Falling agricultural prices forced the owners of small- and medium-sized holdings to sell their land, thus reducing them to the status of tenant farmers.[13]

The drop in prices persisted from the 1660s until 1690, when the prices of cereal, wine, and oil skyrocketed, but that rise came too late to help the wine industry, where prices had fallen the most. The decline in wine production was mirrored by a decline in grain production that lasted half a century. The rise in prices was fueled by poor harvests, caused in part by wet summers and cold winters, as well as by the devaluation created by the Great Powers' financing of the war effort. The drought that began in 1680 devastated an already impoverished countryside. In 1683 the king's agents reported that the wells were dry from March to September. In 1685 and 1686 the peasants faced yet another catastrophe as grasshoppers devoured the corn. Seven years of drought were followed by a cycle of rot during which the grains did not germinate. The peasants also saw the grapevines and olive trees freeze during the hard winters. Climatic disasters only exacerbated the existing structural problems, which caused the collapse of the family economy based on cereal production. Although output plummeted, the importation of grain meant that prices were not affected. The peasant faced ruin, caught between poor harvests and low prices. Between

1700 and 1710 "the entire range of food crop production collapsed at once, like a geological formation."[14]

Many abandoned their homes. Others saw their land and goods, even their windows and doors, seized and sold at auction. The burden of debts and arrears forced taxpayers to abandon their holdings. The taxes, however, were still owed and were levied on those who remained. The unproductive haunted the productive: "The dead clung to the living." In 1703, 70 percent of the first installment of the poll tax was still unpaid in Languedoc. The additional burden on those still producing led to further indebtedness and additional flights, an unending spiral. In the period from 1690 to 1720 the *Wüstungen*, or abandoned sites, mirrored the problems of a society beset by both an agricultural and a demographic crisis.

The demographic crisis aggravated the economic one.[15] The fall in the gross product triggered a subsistence crisis, for the peasant was not only the producer but the principal consumer.[16] Demographically, France entered a period of decline beginning in 1685 or 1690. Many died of malnutrition or its effects. Those who survived subsisted on millet, turnips, and spring vegetables. The most desperate ate acorns or grass bread, made of couch grass and sheep entrails. Those who had wheat shipped it and ate maize instead. Malaria further reduced the poorly clothed, undernourished population. Improverishment, joblessness, poverty, chronic undernourishment, and, only incidentally, late marriage and contraception triggered further depopulation. Many fled to the towns or joined the army, aggravating the labor shortage in the countryside. Between 50 and 90 percent of those who remained needed supplementary income in order to survive. Many worked in the textile industry, which generated more revenue than the grain trade.[17] These disastrous and inescapable conditions were visible manifestations of a severe crisis in rural France. The peasant was caught in a vicious spiral of declining or static production. The revocation of the Edict of Nantes accelerated the existing stagnation, tearing away the economic foundations of the society; it meant the ruin of the silk industry of the Cévennes and the adjacent region, it provoked the flight of capital from Nîmes, and it caused the emigration of many Protestant landowners.

The king enforced his fiscal demands upon an impoverished people facing the inevitable limits of expansion in a preindustrial society. Fiscal exactions along with diminution of profit made them desperate. The pressures of a country at war had then exacerbated the existing economic crisis and perhaps affected the timing of the revolt. Yet the intendant Basville does not mention one word about a fiscal revolt except to worry that the Catholics will use the troubles as an excuse not to pay the *capitation*.[18] Furthermore, the revolt broke out in the more prosperous Cévennes. Some of the insurgents, like Jacques Bonbonnoux, were free of all debt. Bonbonnoux had been able to repay his wife's dowry and leave a small shop and land valued at 250 livres when he joined the rebellion.[19]

What was remarkable was not that the revolt began but that it had not begun earlier. Despair had armed the people. Persecution and massacre had galvanized the Huguenots, who adopted the cry "Liberty of conscience or death!" For many it became just that—a struggle to the death. The government's attempts to eradicate Calvinism had begun in 1661 and culminated with the revocation of the Edict of Nantes in 1685. Louis XIV had moved from limited toleration to legal and finally violent persecution. But the Huguenots were fighting back. In August 1683 the king's agent reported that a number of Huguenots in the Vivarais had purchased weapons and ammunition and had organized companies. They showed, he warned, "every sign of intending to resist the king's troops."[20] Louis's representative in Languedoc argued that "if subjects have a different religion from that of their prince, his dominance and their subjection cannot be complete."[21] Protestantism caused divisions within the state; the spiritual schism could only produce civil schism. This intolerance produced civil war; this belief became self-fulfilling. Louis's policy of establishing Catholicism as the only religion of the state had disastrous consequences in the Cévennes. It led to the destruction of all Calvinist churches, the prohibition of all assemblies, and forced attendance of all children at Mass. The edict was strictly enforced in Languedoc, a bastion of Protestantism and an area with a tradition of revolt against ecclesiastical despotism, an area that had witnessed the Waldensian schism and the Albigensian heresy.

The attempts to extirpate Calvinism in the mountainous Cévennes, where 90 percent belonged to the Reformed faith, meant an attack on the culture of the area.[22] Religion and the synodal structure had forged a communal spirit. The Huguenots formed a highly cohesive, even insular subculture, a society within the larger one, *un contre état calviniste*.[23] Calvinism had permeated the life of the people to such an extent that it had virtually eliminated the native folklore. Psalms replaced the old folksongs and were even sung to lull children to sleep. The use of the *langue d'oïl* in the Bible, in the Protestant texts, and in the church services further reinforced the Protestant sense of community and accentuated the differences with their Catholic neighbors. When the Huguenot mystics spoke in tongues, they spoke in French, not in the *langue d'oc* of the region. Ironically, these Protestants, whom contemporaries viewed as fighting the absolute state, helped to unify the realm through their adoption of the French language. Not only language but also names distinguished the Huguenot community. The Protestants chose names from the Old Testament, such as Élie, Abraham, David, Daniel, Gédéon, and so on.[24] Even jewelry divided the two worlds. The Catholics wore a cross. The Protestants, who considered wearing the cross idolatrous, adopted a symbol of the Holy Spirit. The very insulation of the Calvinists protected their core values and bred an isolationist mentality. The revocation then meant a deculturation, a deculturation enforced by an occupying army.

The military occupation initially ensured that the resistance to the government's edict would remain passive. Many Calvinist ministers insisted on obedience to the sovereign, arguing that the harsh winter and difficult summer before the revocation presaged the persecution. The persecution itself was seen as a sign of the punishment of God. At the outset, the opposition, albeit clandestine, centered in the family, for Protestants the school of faith. It was here that the father read the Bible and intoned the Psalms. The parents reinforced the children's faith. Élie Marion, one of the leaders of the revolt, later reported that the secret instructions of his parents deepened his "aversion for the idolatry and for the errors of Papism."[25] Jean Cavalier emphasized that his mother instructed him in the Scriptures.[26] Some of these children, burdened by feelings of guilt, resented the outward conformity to the edict. Many carried to church books that were ostensibly Catholic texts but were actually Calvinist prayers. Others practiced free marriage rather than go through the Catholic ceremony; they married by mutual consent, without priest, without witnesses. Catholic baptism was often followed by another Protestant baptism. The dying often refused Extreme Unction. But Catholic revenge did not stop at death. Those who had refused the last sacrament were dragged through the mire, face to the ground, and thrown on a refuse heap.[27] Often bodies, secretly buried, were disinterred. Such posthumous vengeance proved so unpopular that more and more Protestants were allowed to die in peace. Only threats filled the churches.

In 1685 the king appointed a new intendant for Languedoc, Basville, a man of inflexible severity and missionary zeal who soon filled the prisons and the galleys. Basville was unlikely to repeat the mistakes of his predecessor, who had been accused of weakness.[28] Indeed, the duc de Saint-Simon portrayed Basville as "a person who above all sought power, who broke any resistance, and for whom no cost was too great, since he was willing to use any means whatsoever"—an implacable man who used power "ruthlessly."[29] This was the man who represented the king in Languedoc for thirty-three years. The Huguenots, in his eyes, were guilty of both heresy and rebellion. For him Protestantism was a "source of dissension and discord." Thus he rigidly adhered to the governmental policy of assimilation, *"un même roi, une même loi, une même foi."* After expelling eighty-five pastors in order to ensure that the Protestants would remain leaderless, he reported, "there is no parish which has not been cleansed."[30] Basville advocated terror in the conviction that it discouraged rebellion. He seized children, billeted troops, closed churches, executed entire families, and interned many in prisons or galleys. The royal troops executed others regardless of sex or age, as they knelt in the woods intoning the Psalms. Even a zealous Catholic contemporary thought that such measures, instead of intimidating the Protestants, stiffened their resolve and created martyrs.[31] Basville himself had his doubts. In one instance he wrote, "these people are so crazy and stupid that I'm afraid they won't remember [the punishment] very long."[32] In an ironic way Basville became another victim of the revocation. As the insurrection continued, he became disillusioned with "this sad life."[33] The government's policy alienated the population, contributing to the milieu that fostered prophetism.

Resistance became more open. People refused to attend the Catholic church and turned instead to the clandestine church, to what became known as the church of the desert. The desert served as a two-edged metaphor indicating both the geography and the spiritual desolation of the Huguenots in France.[34] In 1700 one observer counted sixty regular assemblies.[35] This alone attested to the failure of the Catholics to win over the majority in this region. The clandestine church encompassed both the violent and the resigned; some congregated together to pray, others to arm themselves against the royal dragoons. The Huguenots even contacted the king's enemies during the War of the League of Augsburg in 1689 and 1690 and again during the War of the Spanish Succession. Those who hoped to soften the religious intransigence of Louis XIV with the aid of the Maritime Powers—England and the United Provinces—would be cruelly disappointed by the Treaty of Ryswick in 1697 and the Peace of Utrecht in 1713.

The active struggle of the Huguenots against oppression was influenced by various prophets, including Pierre Jurieu in his *Pastoral Letters*. His vision was a millenarian one that followed the successive stages of the Apocalypse. For him the revocation represented the persecution of the righteous. Papism, he predicted, would end between 1710 and 1720. The Second Coming would follow. Many of the leaders such as Cavalier were familiar with his writings, which were widely disseminated throughout the Cévennes.[36] Just such prophetic logic would dominate the revolt. To those living in expectation of a miracle, the reports of miracles were easily believed—psalms falling from the sky, drums mysteriously beating, trumpets sounding. Natural credulity made them even more receptive to such reports. Their interpretation of the Bible, particularly the Apocalypse, reinforced their belief that God would miraculously intervene. Because the initial prophecies often spoke of agricultural calamities, the subsistence crisis helped fulfill expectations of an Apocalypse.[37] The faithful spoke of destroying the empire of the devil, of the Beast, of the false prophet; they denounced the Catholic authorities in apocalyptic language as "followers of the Beast." Mazel, the prophet in our initial murder, had prophesied the destruction of the empire of the Beast in 1702, by which time the apocalyptic mentality had spread throughout the Cévennes. The authorities, especially the rational Basville, were stupefied by the religious hysteria, convulsions, and so on which they had unleashed. The forced deculturation led to traumatic shock. In the words of Le Roy Ladurie:

The traumatism of a people deprived of its ministers and its spiritual leadership, tormented by a sense of guilt (for having accepted the Revocation and temporarily repudiated its faith) and oppressed in the bargain by hard times and taxes was so severe that it engendered cases of anxiety, neurosis and even hysteria which would turn into bloody fanaticism.[38]

Mazel, for example, could speak of renouncing "idolatry." Bonbonnoux was so haunted by his "sins" that he could not work or sleep or even eat. Both he and his wife regretted that they had gone to a Catholic church to be married.[39] Such feelings of guilt or of deep contrition led to prophetism.

The first visionary was a young shepherdess of sixteen, Isabeau Vincent of the Dauphiné. Baptized a Catholic, she returned to the Protestant faith of her parents.[40] While asleep in 1688 she sang the Ten Commandments in rhyme and then a psalm and finally enjoined the Huguenots to remain true to the faith in the belief that God would save not only her but others as well. Her imprisonment came too late to stop the spread of imitators, who went through the traditional stages of fainting, swooning, convulsions, temporary paralysis, and stiffness or rigidity.[41] A contemporary eyewitness, Mathieu Boissier, wrote an account of his contact with a visionary.

I thought I was listening to an angel. . . . I was forced to believe that there was something in her that was not human. . . . She recited so many passages from the Old and New Testament it was as though she knew the entire Bible by heart.[42]

Such manifestations convinced not only the visionaries but others as well that the Holy Spirit protected them. The visionaries of the Vivarais, believing themselves invulnerable, met a tragic end. Protected by tiny, white, and needless to say invisible angels, they met the soldiers' muskets with bare chests, shouting "Tartara, back

Satan." They were killed where they stood, three hundred strong, in February 1689. Even such massacres did not stop the movement or destroy the faith that existed in families and in isolated villages and hamlets. The prophecies of a Marie la Boiteuse reflected the resiliency of a faith that had not died. In 1700 she announced that the day of deliverance had arrived. She was a little early.

Messianism spread southward to the Cévennes. Many of the visionaries there howled like dogs or crowed like cocks. One, appropriately named Esprit Séguier, had been a companion of Mazel.[43] A neurotic, condemned in his youth for rape, he was caught, tortured, and condemned to be burned. At the stake he tore off his hand, which had been half severed by the executioner, with his teeth. A man like General Villars would label them "lunatics," but few called them impostors.[44] The image of lunacy was reinforced by the constant illusions from the Old Testament, which many found incomprehensible. Furthermore, many prophets were insensible to torture and continued to fantasize to the end. In Jung's words these fantasies or dreams were "streams of imagery" that inspired religious reflection.[45] For the prophets of the eighteenth century, and even those of the twentieth, such religious experiences served as "weapons against humiliation and despair."[46] Numbering perhaps one hundred, these illiterate men and women were mostly peasants and artisans who had turned away from the apostasy of their fathers. We can hear them denounce the treason and cowardice of their parents in the words of one of the leaders, Cavalier, who resolved to "defend the cause of the law that our fathers have unhappily forsaken by cowardice." After hearing that his father had adopted the Catholic faith, Cavalier told him that he had paid too dearly for his freedom—with the loss of his soul. "I would," he argued, "choose prison rather than damn myself." His father should, Cavalier insisted, "shun idolatry" and return to the faith.[47] The cousin of Cavalier testified that he felt a "real hatred for all the pomp of the papists and especially for this farce of the mass. I was not able to see," he continued, "their churches without shuddering."[48] Élie Marion felt a "horror of the idolatry and impiety" of the Catholics and resolved to destroy the "enemies of God."[49] What is striking is the youth of the visionaries.[50] The youngest were seven and fifteen. Isabeau Vincent had visions at seventeen. Mazel, the murderer of the abbot, was twenty-three in 1702. Marion was twenty-four in 1703. Yet another leader, Bonbonnoux, became involved when he was only seventeen after his wife, imprisoned for her faith, died of a disease contracted in jail.[51] Her death transformed him into a rebel, consecrated to God. Among the prophets were the future leaders of the revolt, Cavalier, Mazel, and Roland.

Some have argued that the serious disorganization of the society induced by deculturation resulted in considerable stress, which interfered "with the normal processes of maturation and a secure sense of personal identity."[52] The argument that religious conversion represented one way of overcoming such stress tends by definition to underplay the genuine religious feeling of these people. Furthermore, it pejoratively classifies the rebels as "immature." Certainly the oppression and helplessness so characteristic of adult conversions was also present in the Cévennes. That very experience often produced strong leaders. So too did the death or imprisonment of a relative. Pierre Laporte, dubbed Roland, was inspired by the death of his uncle, Gédéon Laporte. Those normally mute—the young and the women—became prophets. Women like Marie Mathieu, Marie la Boiteuse, Françoise Arbousse, Isabeau Peras, Isabeau Surville, and Françoise Brès played an active role as prophetesses and Camisards. One historian, in his discussion of other women prophets, has argued that visions enabled women to overcome the disabilities of being a female, to get themselves heard by capitalizing on the Christian tradition of holy women.[53]

Le Roy Ladurie argues that most of these women lost their visions when they married, lending credence to the argument that sexual frustration played a role. Such visions, he believes, occurred in a society where sexual mores were ascetic, demanding, and interiorized.[54] But an English agent contends in his memoirs that women continued to preach without the consent of their husbands, brothers, and children.[55] Is Le Roy Ladurie swallowing a commonly held misconception about virginity? Were the Catholics' sexual mores so different from those of the Protestants? For whatever reasons, prophetism, present since 1685, became contagious, as did both individual and collective hysteria.

The role of the prophets in the insurrection was central.[56] As "vessels of the Spirit" they aroused the Protestants from "the sleep of the dead."[57] Jean Cavalier contended that "our inspirations were our recourse and our support."[58] Another prophet, Durand Fage, recounts that visions guided the Camisards. One such prophecy revealed the existence of a traitor, who was later beheaded.[59] If some questioned the sanity of the prophets, none doubted their missionary zeal. The forced abjuration of faith and culture induced a traumatism, a canalizing or channeling of violence into other outlets. The convulsions and visions were a concrete way to express this trauma. Such hysterical phenomena were culturally patterned.[60] Clary, one of the prophets, placed himself "under God's protection.... Finally I commit[ted] all to God." Roland heard a "call to rise from God."[61] Élie Marion shed tears of blood.[62] Cavalier wrote that he "was driven by a force above me."[63] In assemblies many heard voices in the air or trumpets; others spoke in tongues or saw angels. Still others engaged in sexual exhibitionism or collective masochism. In a celebrated instance of public penitence, women tore out their hair. As has been said of another revolt, "in the social drama, all the actors were playing to two audiences, one in this world and one in the next."[64] "Bodily movement and gesture without speech," a historian of modern France suggests, "was the language used to assert the cohesion of the community."[65] Such rituals both expressed community cohesion and created it. Rituals "in the sense of a stereotyped sequence of actions" not only served as symbols; they also highlighted the grievances and legitimated the violence, transforming murders into executions.[66] Such actions were but another part of a multifaceted reaction to forced deculturation, to apostasy. The visionaries were only the most visible manifestation of this crisis.

Such visions, such public hysteria, not only engendered courage and confidence but strengthened the rebels' conviction that they were on the side of God.[67] After the murder of the abbot, resistance crystallized around a group of young chiefs, and the number of insurgents multiplied. As summer became fall, the agitation became a revolt. The priests fled to the protection of the cities. The clandestine church supported the Camisards, whose fighting faith, strict discipline, prophecy, and inspiration earned their movement the sobriquet "théâtre sacré." One royalist commander on being surprised cried out, "À vous voici, messieurs les fanatiques!"[68] When fighting they would often intone the psalms, especially Psalm 68:

> God arises, his enemies are scattered and they who hate him flee from before his face. As smoke is scattered, so they are scattered; as wax melts away before the fire so sinners perish before God. But the just rejoice. ... Sing to God, sing a psalm to his name; make ready a path for him who is borne through the desert.... The Lord gives the word; the joyful crowd of messengers is great: "The kings of the armies are fleeing, fleeing; and the inhabitants of the house divide the spoils."... Our God is the God who saves, and the Lord God gives deliverance from death. Indeed God crushes the heads of his enemies.... God is to be feared from his sanctuary, the God of Israel; he gives power and strength to his people.

But the just did not rejoice, nor were their enemies scattered. Psalm 69 proved to be a more apt and more chilling portent:

> Save me, O God, for the waters have come up to my neck. I am stuck fast in the mire of the deep, and there is nowhere to set my foot. I am come into deep waters, and the waves overwhelm me. I have grown weary of crying, my throat has become hoarse; my eyes have failed while I await my God. More numerous than the hairs of my head are they who hate me without cause, stronger than my bones are they who unjustly oppose me: shall I return that which I took not away?

After this catalog of misery the psalm advocates punishment for the persecutors.

> Let their eyes be darkened that they see not, and make their loins continually to shake. Pour out thine indignation upon them.... and let there be none to dwell in their tents.... Let them be blotted out of the book of the living and let them not be enrolled among the just.

These visionaries, unlike the Muggletonians of England, preached war, not peace: "Burn the churches; kill the Catholics." It became a holy war. The primitive savagery and ritual murders that characterized the revolt led contemporaries to label it the savage rebellion. Rebels, for example, tore the fetuses from the wombs of Catholic peasant women and threatened to burn alive peasants who attended Mass. In God's name they pillaged and murdered priests. The official royal accounts emphasized their savagery, the Camisard accounts their strict discipline and piety. Certainly a number of sensational incidents attributed to the insurgents by governmental sources may have been committed by local scoundrels under cover of the rebellion.[69] Nonetheless, the government could not ignore the rebels as their numbers mushroomed from an initial eighty to twelve hundred in 1700 and ultimately to five thousand.

The Catholic propagandists dubbed them fanatics, villains, bandits, rogues, and scoundrels. The Protestants called them insurrectionists, malcontents, even martyrs and heroes. Who were they? The Camisards came predominantly from the peasant and artisan classes, 42 and 58 percent respectively. Most of the artisans worked in the wool trade as *cardeurs, peigneurs*, or *tisserands* (carders, combers, or weavers). One Pierre Laporte, called Roland (b. 1680) was a *châtreur de moutons*, another, Cavalier (b. 1681) a baker's aide.[70] Generally, neither the bourgeoisie nor the nobility actively participated in the insurrection, but women and children did. Aping the nobility, leaders often dressed in theatrical costumes. One, for example, dressed in a red cloak and rode a white horse. Cavalier stripped his fallen adversaries and donned their noble garb. Such theatrical gestures helped to mobilize the populace behind certain individuals, such as the blond-haired, blue-eyed Cavalier, and to provide a rallying point in the ensuing melees. The mythogenic identification with the Camisard leaders suggests, as Peter Burke has posited about outlaws, that they "satisfied repressed wishes, enabling ordinary people to take imaginative revenge on the authorities to whom they were usually obedient in real life."[71]

The king dispatched four regiments to quell the insurrection, but the terrain of the area and the complicity of the populace made the intendant's task a formidable one. Basville, for one, complained that the inaccessibility and the remoteness of this land, "the most wretched in the world," made the populace more likely to rebel.[72] The Rhône and the mountains isolated the movement, delineating an area where wild highlands rose to central mountains, a region particularly suitable for guerrilla warfare. The raiders would disappear into villages and gather supplies at night. In most battles the rebels did not number more than fifteen hundred, but their realization that the punishment they faced if caught was worse than death inspired them to fight ferociously and give no quarter. When outnumbered they would melt into the countryside. Their mobility and their knowledge of the area gave them an enormous advantage. The rebels divided into several groups, each with its own secret cache of provisions. Not united in any formal way, they proved an elusive enemy. The maréchal de Montrevel, the commander of the government troops, thought it "une espèce de miracle" to encounter them. It was no use, he said, to try to find those "invisible demons." Basville, exasperated with Montrevel's inaction and his strategy, denounced him as incompetent and foolish.[73] To put down what had become a popular and peasant uprising the government attempted to intimidate through execution or through razing several villages. The rebels replied in kind with other atrocities. The government's repression merely cemented the solidarity between the Camisards and the population. Cavalier contended that the government's failure to distinguish between the innocent and the guilty engendered an insecurity that led men to support the Camisard cause.[74] The authorities found themselves caught in a vicious cycle: increasing the number of troops might only add to the number of insurgents.

By 1703 the beleaguered Montrevel was proposing desperate solutions, such as a scorched-earth policy.[75] He intended to destroy the countryside, to level the villages, to demolish the ovens and mills in order to ensure that the rebels died of cold and hunger, to rid the country of this "vermin" which continued to multiply. Basville, however, insisted on following the law in keeping the distinction between the innocent and the guilty. He rejected Montrevel's proposal to take hostages and execute two for every one Catholic killed.[76] Meanwhile some of the Catholics, who had decided to defend themselves, sewed onto their garments small white crosses. These *Camisards blancs, Cadets de la Croix*, or *florentins* soon began to terrorize the local populations, adding to the insecurity and anarchy of the countryside. Various accounts reinforced Cavalier's argument that the *Camisards blancs* were "capable of more atrocious cruelties than one can imagine."[77] Even Montrevel turned against this brigandage and issued an edict against them. In September 1703 he launched a program of deportation, massacre, summary judgment, and destruction of homes and provisions.[78] After razing 466 villages, he regrouped the people in walled areas or strategic hamlets, threatening them with death if they attempted to return to their former villages. Many died of starvation or fatigue en route; others died in cells or galleys. Even Cavalier's threat to burn two villages for every one Montrevel burned did not stop the destruction. Finding one prophet and his followers, the royalists executed all seventy of them. Basville was appalled at the summary execution of unarmed men: "I have never seen anything more horrible than this butchery in cold blood."[79] They could well have intoned with the psalmist, *Save me, O God, for the waters have come up to my neck.*

Too late to save his brethren, Jean Cavalier counterattacked at Sommières, burning inns, massacring Catholics, stealing supplies, and destroying granaries, mills, sheds, even sheep pens. The young Cavalier, general of the *armée des fidèles*, a man less impulsive and more calculating than Roland, swore vengeance before a bloody trophy, the head of one of the rebels. *Let their dwellings be devastated and let there be none to dwell in their tents.* The "vengeance of heaven" was heavy: forty churches burned or pillaged, between two hundred and three hundred abandoned, two hundred inhabitants killed.[80] Such violence united, integrated. The early harsh winter aggravated the misery of the countryside.[81] Atrocities followed atrocities. Royalists killed prisoners taken. In one engagement, rebels pulled a royalist from his horse and beheaded him. On 26 February 1703 yet another rebel, André Castanet, avenging the death of his mother and sister, took the village of Fraissinet-de-Fourques and executed all the inhabitants, including women and children. *Let them be blotted out of the book of the living.*

By 1704 the rebels had no refuge; they faced cold, famine, despair, a descent into hell. *I am stuck fast in the mire of the deep and there is nowhere to set foot.* The Cévennes had been systematically devastated by fire. In March 1704 the rebels, by now reckless, ambushed a group of royal troops, killing twenty-two officers and three hundred soldiers. Their commander had enjoined them, "My brothers, double your prayers and we will be the victors."[82] They were. They despoiled the dead, taking the plumed hats and embroidered jerkins and donning them. *Let their eyes be darkened that they see not.*

The appointment in April 1704 of Claude Louis Hector de Villars signaled a new policy of pacification. He might well have commented, as had his successor, that he "came not as a persecutor, nor as a missionary, but in the resolution to render justice equally to all the world."[83] He believed that the cruelty had only prolonged the conflict. In March the revolt was at its height, but three months later the most important rebels had submitted, and two months after that the majority of the Camisards. Villars continued to pursue the rebels vigorously while at the same time extending offers of amnesty. Fortunately for Villars, just before his arrival a soldier spotted an old woman carrying food. Threatened with hanging, she finally divulged the location of the rebels' provisions. The royalists then proceeded to the cache, surprising some thirty rebels, killing them, and sticking their ears upon bayonets. They went on to massacre the population of the neighboring villages. *I am come into deep waters and the waves overwhelm me.* By 19 April Villars had encircled the partisans, surprising Cavalier's men in a skirmish and killing a third of them, including three prophetesses. None asked for quarter. They sought death, the royalists reported, "with an extraordinary ferocity."

Now with a stronger hand, Villars could play the role of pacifier. He removed the scaffolds and the torture wheels from the villages. If the rebels came down from the forest and the mountains, they would be offered amnesty. They could leave the country or join the king's army on the condition that they be dispersed throughout the royal forces. Louis was certainly anxious for a settlement. Although the royalists had succeeded in isolating and containing the revolt, the war had threatened Louis's position. He was forced to commit troops to a rear-guard action at the same time he was fighting most of Europe in the War of the Spanish Succession. On his part Cavalier, dispirited and certainly weary of the killings, had no more hope of any human aid. The daring Roland told Cavalier that he would rather die than place himself in the mouth of a lion.[84]

Cavalier could not agree. In May 1704 Cavalier signed a humble letter to the king requesting pardon and asking that the partisans be allowed to leave the realm.[85] As he signed, did he remember another abjuration, an earlier one signed by his father, one he had so vigorously denounced? *I have grown weary of crying, my throat has become hoarse.* Cavalier was offered a command in the royal army and vague promises of toleration for his co-religionists, promises later violated with impunity. He did enter the royal army but later escaped and fought with the allies. A company of refugees under his leadership attempted to reach Languedoc through Catalonia. Most of the company was decimated at the battle of Almanza, and Cavalier was left for dead. After recovering, he joined an expedition with the duke of Savoy in southeastern France. He later served as governor of the isle of Jersey. In a poignant letter to a friend in 1738 he quoted the psalm he had often intoned with his comrades.[86] He never returned to France. He died in 1740 in Chelsea on a trip to London.

Many other French refugees faced the enmity of the Huguenot clergy throughout Europe, who regarded them as fanatics or charlatans. The synod in Switzerland, for example, refused to allow Castanet to preach. Marion went to England. While on a mission to the continent in 1713 he was arrested by officers of the Polish army as a Swedish spy. Although he was eventually released eight months later, he was mortally ill from a fever caught in Poland and died on the way to Rome in November of that year.[87] Bonbonnoux lived the life of a fugitive, with the earth as his bed and the heavens his roof until 1730 when he fled to Switzerland, where he died in 1755. The French prophets in exile "lived in a Cévenol past and the wide millennial kingdom of the future. When the last French prophet died a certain world did end."[88] The majority, however, did not survive. Many, knowing only violence, continued the fight. *More numerous than the hairs of my head are those who hate me.*

At this point, when it was too late, Tobie de Rocayrol, an allied agent, promised aid. Even he would later betray them. Roland fought on until 1704, when a traitor divulged his location for one hundred louis. *I have become a stranger to my brethren.* Even then he managed to escape from the chateau, which had been surrounded by government forces while he slept. The troops followed and surrounded him, but he fought so fiercely that they were unable to take him alive.[89] A guardsman shot him at point-blank range. He was then twenty-four years old. His companions were captured and broken on the wheel. Roland was posthumously condemned for *lèse majesté* and open rebellion. The authorities dragged his body through the mire and burned it under the scaffold where his comrades had been hanged. The ashes were scattered to the winds. The death of the intrepid and indefatigable Roland on 14 August helped to end any hope the combatants might have cherished.[90]

Individuals and groups gradually surrendered. The autonomy of the partisans, which had initially worked to their advantage, now worked against them, for they did not present a united front when they negotiated with the king's agents. Most preferred exile. The majority of the chiefs surrendered by October 1704. A few continued to resist throughout 1705.[91] After returning from Switzerland, Castanet was taken and broken on the wheel.[92] In 1706 Catinat and Ravanel were surrounded, reclothed in chemises coated with sulfur, attached to rings of iron, and burned at the stake. The rebels continued the fight until 1710 with no munitions, no allies, and no friends to aid them.[93] It was a desperate and doomed struggle. Mazel, our initial murderer, had obtained an amnesty and gone into exile in 1704. When he returned to France, he was arrested and condemned to perpetual imprisonment. He escaped with sixteen others and was again pardoned, given a passport, and escorted to the frontier. He fared less well on his second return. After living in Geneva, Holland, and then again in Geneva he reentered France in 1709 to rejoin his comrades and to instigate a new insurrection. He did not live a year. In 1710 he was captured and killed. His head was burned in the public square at Vernoux. *I have become disheartened and have waited for someone to take pity, but there was no one, and for comforters, but I found none.*

NOTES

1. A number of contemporary accounts illumine the revolt: Jacques Bonbonnoux, *Mémories de Bonbonnoux, chef Camisard et pasteur du desert* (Cévennes, 1883); Jean Cavalier, *Mémoires*; Maximilien Mission, *Le Théâtre sacre des Cévennes* (Marseilles, 1977); *Mémoires inédit d'Abraham Mazel et d'Élie Marion sur la guerre des Cévennes, 1701–1708*, vol. 34 of *The Publications of the Huguenot Society of London* (Paris, 1931); *Méslange de littérature, historique et critique sur tout qui regarde l'état extraordinaire des Cévennois* (London, 1707); *Nouveaux mémoires pour servir à l'histoire des trois Camisards* (London 1708); *Examen du Theâtre sacré des Cévennes* [in English, *Cry from the Desert*] (London, 1708). Part of this chapter has appeared in *The Proceedings of the Western Society for French History* 13 (1986).

2. H. de Villenoisy, "L'Abbé du Cherla, monstre sadistique ou martyr de la foi," *Almanach cévenol* 5:73–87.

3. See Mission, ed., *Le Théâtre sacré*, pp. 143–145, for Mazel's own account.

4. The Catholics compared him to Saint Sebastian and the revolt to a new jacquerie, led by bandits without faith, without law. *Précis historique de la guerre des Camisards, 1702–1710* (Nîmes, 1892), pp. 14, 47, 62.

5. Mission, ed., *Le Théâtre sacré*, p. 144–145.

6. Jean-Robert Armogathe and Philippe Joutard, "Bâville et la guerre des Camisards," *Revue d'historie moderne et contemporaine* 19 (1972):51.

7. Mazel gives us this explanation. Quoted in Philippe Joutard, ed., *Les Camisards* (Paris, 1976), p. 111.

8. Pierre Goubert, "Les Cadres de la vie rurale," in *Histoire économique et sociale de la France* by Ernst Labrousse et al. (Paris, 1970), 2:87–118.

9. Robin Briggs, *Early Modern France, 1560–1715* (New York, 1977), p. 52.

10. Charles Tilly, *The Contentious French* (Cambridge, Mass., 1986), pp. 134 and 171.

11. Pierre Goubert, "Le Paysan et la terre: Seigneurie, tenure, exploitation," in Labrousse, *Histoire économique* 2:147, hereafter cited as Goubert, "Le Paysan et la terre."

12. Briggs, *Early Modern France*, p. 39.

13. Pierre Goubert, "Le 'Tragique' XVIIe siècle," in Labrousse, *Histoire économique*, p. 341.

14. Le Roy Ladurie, *The Peasants of Languedoc* (Chicago, 1974), p. 231.

15. Pierre Goubert, "Le Régime démographique français au temps de Louis XIV," in Labrousse, *Histoire économique* 2:23–54.

16. Jean Meuvret, *Le Problème des subsistances à l'époque Louis XIV: La Production des céréales dans la France du XVIIe et du XVIIIe siècle* (The Hague, 1977), 1:45.

17. Tihomir J. Markovitch, *Les Industries lainières de Colbert à la Révolution* (Geneva, 1976), p. 457; and Pierre Goubert, "Le Paysan et la terre," p. 147.

18. Armogathe and Joutard, "Bâville," p. 55.

19. Philippe Joutard, ed., *Journaux Camisards (1700–1715)* (Paris, 1965), p. 8.

20. Tilly, *The Contentious French*, p. 155.

21. Quoted in Pierre Miquel, *Les Guerres de religion* (Paris, 1980), p. 487.

22. Basville claimed that in Languedoc there were about 198,483 Protestants out of a total population of approximately 1.5 million. The Protestants were more heavily concentrated in the mountains, an area so

impenetrable that it "makes the inhabitants seditious and inclined to rebellion." Tilly, *The Contentious French*, p. 168.

23. Janine Garrisson-Estebe, *L'Homme protestante* (Paris, 1980), p. 7.

24. Philippe Joutard, *La Légende des Camisards: Une sensibilité au passé* (Paris: Gallimard, 1977), p. 39.

25. Miquel, *Les guerres de religion*, p. 495.

26. Cavalier, *Memoires*, p. 33.

27. Ibid., p. 492.

28. "Si les voies douces sont tournées en poison, il faut bien, malgré l'inclination naturelle en reprendre de severes ou laisser tout perdre." Armogathe and Joutard, "Bâville," p. 61.

29. Tilly, *The Contentious French*, p. 170.

30. Miguel, *Les Guerres de religion*, p. 419. See Nicolas Lamoignon de Bâville, *Mémoires pour servir a l'histoire de Languedoc* (Amsterdam, 1734).

31. G. Paysan, *Les Camisards da Vivarais* (Le Mazel Banne, 1981), p. 80–82.

32. Tilly, *The Contentious French*, p. 155.

33. "Le métier d'intendant est si triste maintenant . . . je n'y ai trouvé que véritables sujets d'inquiétude, des difficultés a surmonter sans fin, aucun moment de repos et de tranquillité et j'ai oublié entièrement la douceur qu'il y a posseder son âme en paix qui devroit être le seul bonheur de la vie." Bâville, 25 May 1708. Quoted by Armogathe and Joutard, "Bâville,"p. 62.

34. Hillel Schwartz, *The French Prophets: The History of a Millenarian Group in Eighteenth-Century England* (Berkeley, Calif., 1980), p. 14.

35. Miquel, *Les Guerres de religion*, p. 495.

36. Cavalier, *Mémoires*, p. 40.

37. Joutard, *Les Camisards*, pp. 32, 59, and 86.

38. Ladurie, *The Peasants of Languedoc*, p. 272.

39. Joutard, ed., *Journaux Camisards*, pp. 29 and pp. 118–119.

40. Miquel, *Les Guerres de religion*, p. 497, and Paysan, *Les Camisards*, pp. 72–73.

41. A contemporary writer, David Augustin, argued according to the scientific explanation of his day, "Le fanatisme est proprement une maladie de l'esprit ou une espèce de mélancolie et de manie, qui porte ceux qui en sont atteints a se persuader qu'ils ont le pouvoir de faire des miracles et de prophétiser. . . . Les gens mélancoliques et atrabiliaires peuvent aisement tomber dans cette maladie." Paysan, *Les Camisards*, p. 75.

42. Mission, ed, *Le Théâtre sacré*, pp. 62–63. Mission, a Norman Huguenot and friend of the Camisards, published this and other accounts in 1707 to dispel the notion that the Camisards were impostors.

43. A hostile Catholic described him as "un homme de mine affreuse, et d'un visage noir, maigre, long, n'ayant point de dents supérieures." Quoted in Joutard, *La Légende*.

44. Even a writer who explained the revolt as a "maladie spirituelle" did not think the Camisards were impostors. Hippolyte Blanc, *De L'Inspiration des Camisards*, 1859, reprint, (Paris, 1978), pp. 180 and 11.

45. Naomie R. Goldenberg, "Dreams and Fantasies as Sources of Revelation," in *Womanspirit Rising*, edited by Carol P. Christ and Judith Plaskow (new York, 1979), p. 224.

46. Frantz Fanon, *The Wretched of the Earth* (New York, 1966), p. 16.

47. Cavalier, *Mémoires*, p. 47.

48. Mission, ed., *Le Théâtre sacré*, p. 97.

49. Ibid., p. 138.

50. André Dumas, *Le Desert cévenol* (Paris, 1932), p. 178; and Mission, *Le Théâtre sacré*, p. 96.

51. Bonbonnoux, *Mémoires*, pp. 7–11.

52. Guenther Lewy, *Religion and Revolution* (New York, 1974), p. 262.

53. Alfred Cohen, "Prophecy and Madness: Women Visionaries during the Puritan Revolution," *Journal of Psychohistory* 22 (Winter 1984):413.

54. Ladurie, *The Peasants of Languedoc*, p. 285. Schwartz, *The French Prophets*, disagrees with this interpretation.

55. Marquis de Guiscard, *Memoirs* (London, 1705), p. 7.

56. Daniel Vidal, *L'Ablatif absolu, théorie du prophetisme, le discours camisard en Europe, 1706–1713* (Paris, 1977).

57. Robert P. Gagg, *Das Leben der südfranzösischen Hugenottenkirche nach dem Todesurteil durch Ludwig XIV* (Zurich, 1961), p. 165.

58. Mission, ed., *Le Théâtre sacré*, p. 138.

59. Ibid., p. 172–173.

60. Ralph Linton, *Culture and Mental Disorders* (Springfield, Ill., 1956), p. 132.

61. Gagg, *Die Hugenottenkirche*, p. 256.

62. Ibid., p. 265.

63. Mission, ed., *Le Théâtre sacré*, p. 13.

64. Peter Burke, "The Virgin of the Carmine and the Revolt of Masaniello," *Past and Present* 99 (May 1983):20.

65. Theodore Zeldin, *France, 1848–1945, Taste and Corruption* (New York, 1980), p. 309.

66. Ibid., pp. 14–19.

67. Mazel contends, "C'est Dieu, Dieu lui-même, son conseil et son bras qui ont opéré ce que l'esprit humain ne saurait comprendre." Misson, ed., *Le Théâtre sacré*, p. 13.

68. Maurice Pezet, *L'Épopee des Camisards, Languedoc, Vivarais, Cévennes* (Paris, 1978), p. 112.
69. For example, see Cavalier, *Memoires*, p. 169; and Paysan, *Les Camisards*, pp. 177–182 on the murder of Mme. de Mirmand.
70. Arthur Grubb, *Jean Cavalier* (London, 1931).
71. Peter Burke, *Popular Culture in Early Modern Europe* (New York, 1978) p. 166.
72. Bâville, *Mémoires*, pp. 77–81; Joutard, *La Légende*, p. 59.
73. Armogathe and Joutard, "Bâville."
74. Jean Cavalier, *Mémoires sur la guerre des Camisards*, annotated by Frank Puaux (Paris, 1979), p. 60.
75. André Ducasse, *La Guerre des Camisards: La Résistance huguenote sous Louis XIV* (Paris, 1962), p. 129.
76. Armogathe and Joutard, "Bâville."
77. Cavalier, *Mémoires*, p. 148; and Paysan, *Les Camisards*, pp. 173–176.
78. The government inflicted so much damage on parishes in the dioceses of Mende and Uzes that the authorities exempted them from general taxes from 1705 to 1730. Tilly, *The Contentious French*, p. 175.
79. Ibid., p. 63.
80. Miquel, *Les Guerres de religion*, p. 500.
81. André Chamson, *Castanet, le Camisard de l'Aigoual* (Paris, 1979), p. 156.
82. Miquel, *Les Guerres de religion*, p. 504.
83. Berwick, *Mémoires*, 1,179.
84. Cavalier, *Mémoires*, p. 207.
85. Reprinted in Joutard's *Les Camisards*, pp. 187–188.
86. Pezet, *L'Épopee des Camisards*, p. 196.
87. Hillel Schwartz, *The French Prophets* and *Knaves, Fools, Madmen, and that Subtile Effluvium: A Study of the Opposition to the French Prophets in England, 1706–1711* (Gainesville, Fl., 1978).
88. Schwartz, *The French Prophets* (1980), p. 292.
89. B.M., Add. Mss. 61258, fols. 91–92, is a contemporary account of his death dated 17 August 1704.
90. See the vivid recollections of Marion and of Bonbonnoux in Joutard, ed., *Journaux Camisards*, pp. 89–105 and pp. 144–147.
91. B.M., Add. Mss. 61258, fols. 190–201, captures the desperation of the rebels.
92. André Chamson, *Castanet, le Camisard de l'Aigoual* (Paris, 1979).
93. Cavalier, *Mémoires*, p. 207. A special note of thanks must go to Robert Linder for his theological and nocturnal assistance.

3

Hungary

One of the most successful and disruptive insurrections during the War of the Spanish Succession (1702–1714), the "War for Independence" or the Rákóczi revolt broke out in Hungary in 1703. At the turn of the century the Hungarians rebelled against the domination of a foreign power, the Habsburgs, just as the Moldavians, Ukrainians, Livonians, and Poles resisted, although futilely, the Ottomans, Romanovs, Vasas, and Wettins. Foreign absolutism triumphed over noble privilege not only in Hungary but throughout Eastern Europe, an area characterized by the dominance of agriculture and the powerful position of the nobility. The strength of that nobility was coupled inextricably with the region's inability to withstand foreign domination. The entrenched nobility had successfully withstood the establishment of a strong monarchy within their societies but in so doing had virtually ensured their failure to withstand the imposition of absolutism from without; these Eastern European societies lacked not only strong rulers but also viable armies, centralized governments, and strong bureaucracies. When absolutist states moved into these areas they confronted a powerful nobility who led the resistance. From their numbers came Johann Reinhold Patkul, Ivan Mazepa, Stanislaw Lesczynski, Dimitrie Cantemir, and Ferenc Rákóczi II.[1] Rákóczi

(1676–1735), a prince of the Holy Roman Empire and the wealthiest landowner in Hungary,[2] came from an illustrious family, many of whose members had revolted, albeit unsuccessfully, against the Habsburgs: his father, Ferenc Rákóczi I; his mother, Helen Zrínyi; and his stepfather, Imre Thököly. Rákóczi personified, he would later write, the force of his country and the prestige of his ancestors. The Habsburgs, aware of the family's tradition of opposition, took the young Ferenc from his mother, educated him in a Jesuit college, and subsequently married him to a German princess, Charlotte Amalia von Hessen-Rheinfels. This effort seemed initially successful, for in 1697 Rákóczi refused to head an uprising in the Tokay region. Although quickly suppressed, this revolt revealed the extent of dissatisfaction with Habsburg rule, particularly the government's economic policy, which brought ruin to this formerly prosperous area. After 1697 Rákóczi's attitude changed markedly, in part because of his increasing awareness of his heritage and the exploitative nature of Habsburg rule and in part because of his friendship with his neighbor, Count Miklos Bercsényi, an intelligent, ambitious, and articulate foe of the Habsburgs. Rákóczi soon began to plot to overthrow the Habsburgs and, like his predecessors, attempted to obtain the support of foreign powers, most logically Louis XIV of France, Leopold's archrival. Leopold, however, learned of Rákóczi's intrigues and had him imprisoned at Wiener-Neustadt to await almost certain execution. With the help of his wife, Rákóczi staged a daring escape and fled to Poland, where he, along with Bercsényi, attempted to persuade Augustus II to support them, alleging that the Hungarians were "ready to risk all and wait only for the proper moment to act."[3]

Rákóczi soon heard of a revolt that began in 1703 in an area called Tiszáhat among peasants, who were afraid of losing their freedom. Northeastern Hungary proved particularly susceptible to insurrectionary sentiment because of the visible presence of many Habsburg officials and soldiers. The insurrection sparked to life there and fittingly and finally flickered out there. A group of peasants, led by Tamas Esze, successfully appealed to Rákóczi to return to his native country and lead them in the struggle to liberate Hungary from Habsburg rule. Rákóczi in turn called on his fellow countrymen, "all true Hungarians, ecclesiastics and laymen, nobles and commoners, military men and civilians" to fight for "God, Fatherland and Liberty,"[4] to repel the Habsburgs, who were "pillaging, taxing, trampling on our honor, and robbing [us of] our bread and salt" (Brezan patent, 6 May 1703).[5] He described Hungary as a nation that could not "live in slavery" and that did not "fear to die for its liberty."[6] He urged the nobility to join the struggle (Nameny manifesto, 18 July 1703) and thus united two disparate movements, the nobles' resistance to Habsburg absolutism and the popular insurrection.[7] Rákóczi regarded the support of the nobility as crucial. The newly created nobility in western Hungary, who owed their lands and titles to the Habsburgs, remained loyal to the dynasty, as did many who, as Rákóczi observed, feared the people as much as they did the Germans. The old nobility pledged themselves to Rákóczi. Still others found themselves *kurucs* in spite of themselves. Yet others, such as the inhabitants of the *hajdu* towns—military outposts immune from feudal taxes and dues—and other places around important fortifications, roads, or border areas, such as the one between Hungary and Transylvania, feared the loss of their military privileges and tax exemptions after the expulsion of the Turks.[8]

A combination of economic, religious, and social grievances ignited the insurrection in 1703. In that year Rákóczi could take advantage of Leopold I's and later Joseph I's preoccupation with that great struggle in the West, the War of the Spanish Succession, and could capitalize on the military vacuum left by the withdrawal of Austrian troops. The conflict between Rákóczi and the Habsburgs exemplified a regional attempt to stem the growing power of the absolutist state and to retain or recover traditional liberties and privileges. Rákóczi, representing the particularistic interests of the Hungarians, sought to reinstitute Hungary's constitutional liberties, while Leopold strove to establish a centralized empire and increase control from Vienna. Leopold I had conquered Hungary, which had served as a borderland, a no-man's-land, between the Habsburg and Turkfish empires. The Treaty of Karlowitz (1699) confirmed all that Leopold had won in years of warfare with the Turks: all of Transylvania and Hungary up to the Sava-Maros line. But the reconquered lands were underpopulated and impoverished; they had been devastated by the Turks, the border wars, and the occupation troops and decimated by epidemics and famines. Under Habsburg rule conditions had continued to deteriorate for all classes, particularly the serfs.

Leopold's policies toward the newly reconquered lands also served to alienate the nobility and the native peasantry. For example, Vienna quartered large number of ill-disciplined troops in Hungary. Undoubtedly the movement of troops, which entailed the usual requisitioning and abuses, had helped to ignite the conflict. The Hungarians had handed the Habsburgs the perfect pretext to station troops and build up their power there when the Hungarian Diet had agreed in January 1649 to the Habsburg garrisoning of troops along the 150-mile Ottoman border. In spite of vociferous objections, the Habsburgs continued to quarter troops to "protect" the populace. As the Habsburgs frequently said, "whether you like it or not, His Majesty protects you."[9] This protection in the late seventeenth century averaged between twenty-four thousand and sixty-four thousand troops. Through such troops His Majesty could not only protect but also control what one of his ministers referred to as "a nation of rebels, robbers, and restless men."[10] After liberating Buda from the Turks Leopold gave the Hungarians the opportunity to express their "gratitude." At the Diet of Pozsony (October 1687) the Hungarian estates assembled and recognized the hereditary succession of the Habsburgs through the male line and gave up the *ius resistendi*, the right of resistance, held since 1222 (through the decrees of Andrew II). Leopold subsequently disregarded the constitution, breaking the oath that he had taken as king of Hungary. He established a commission, a *commissio neo acquistica*, to validate claims of ex-landowners to land in ex-Ottoman territory or, when that proved impossible, to distribute land to new owners. The emperor, desperately short of funds, saw in the new lands a lucrative source of income, a way of settling old debts or rewarding faithful servants. He often, for example, rented the newly conquered lands to the imperial, not the Hungarian, nobility. Leopold did agree to restore the land to the previous owners, but only after each owner had substantiated his claims—an impossible task owing to the ravages of the war that had destroyed so many records—and paid an indemnity (a *redemtio juris armorum*) equivalent to approximately 10 percent of the value of the land. Many did not have the means to pay the tax or refused to pay it and denounced the whole process as illegal. Others, falsely accused of collusion with the rebel Thököly, saw their property confiscated. Still others saw immigrants granted political, economic, and religious privileges they were denied.

Leopold subsequently granted large areas of Hungary to foreigners. The recently established commission openly vowed to temper the Hungarian blood "with its tendency to unrest and revolution" with German blood so that the kingdom would be "turned thereby to a steadfast loyalty and love of their natural hereditary king."[11] To further strengthen his hold over Hungary Leopold appointed Germans to important Hungarian offices and encouraged both Germans and Serbs to immigrate to the underpopulated areas, granting them preferential treatment through taxes, monopolies, and licenses. Serbs and Germans came flooding into Hungary. The Rascians or Orthodox Serbs, who settled on the military frontiers, enjoyed greater religious freedom than the Hungarian Protestants, paid no manorial dues, and were not subject to local jurisdiction. The Habsburgs protected the Serbs, whom they viewed as a bulwark against both the Turks and the Hungarian malcontents. During the war with Rákóczi the government granted all Orthodox Serbs a privileged position, exempting them, for example, from billeting and other military exactions.[12] This strategy paid off. Lieutenant Field Marshal Maximilian Petrasch, a Serb who commanded the fortress at Brod, correctly predicted that the privileged status of the Serbs guaranteed their loyalty to the Habsburgs and their continued hostility to the Hungarians.[13] In spite of the strenuous efforts of the Hungarians to win over the Serbs in particular to the *kuruc* cause, the Greek Orthodox Serbs and the Catholic Croats were ultimately the only non-Magyar nationalities to remain loyal to the Habsburgs. That loyalty proved worth the price. The Serbs could raise forty thousand men who excelled in mobile warfare. Rákóczi did not underestimate their contribution. Rákóczi, who had hoped to hire them as mercenaries, realized, as he told Louis XIV, that they were "the Germans' only hope" of stopping his advance. In a similar vein, Bercsényi predicted that the Serbs, who were excellent soldiers, would prove to be "quite unpleasant as an enemy."[14] The Serbs and Germans served not only as soldiers but also as tax collectors, increasing the already latent and widespread xenophobia. It is little wonder, then, that the Hungarians resented the Germans and to a lesser extent the Serbs and that hatred of foreign rule played such an important role in the war. Rákóczi reflected that very attitude in his memoirs when he wrote of a Hungary despoiled of her liberties, oppressed by insupportable exactions and taxes, and subject to the domination of a foreign nation. His primary goal was to deliver his country from the foreign yoke, the Habsburg yoke of servitude.[15]

But economic grievances loomed even larger. Leopold's economic policies proved disastrous for not only the nobility but the serfs and burghers as well. Leopold's taxes were levied partially to offset the costs of war. War created a tremendous drain on revenues; the War of the Spanish Succession, for example, cost the government annually about 20 million florins.[16] The oppressive taxes depressed an already impoverished economy, an economy whose role in world trade, particularly in the export of copper and cattle, had markedly decreased.[17] During the agricultural boom of the fifteenth and sixteenth centuries cattle had dominated Hungarian exports to the West. In the sixteenth century cattle had made up between 85 and 90 percent of all exports. The Hungarians had turned to beef because the Hungarian plain was well suited to the raising of cattle and because it was not as labor-intensive as agriculture. The decline in the export of cattle proved particularly devastating to this essentially one-dimensional agrarian economy. During this economic recession the Habsburgs levied not only old taxes but new ones as well, on consumption and inheritance. Monopolies in silver, salt, and cattle in addition to privileges and preemptions meant in effect a greater concentration of wealth and even higher taxes. A citizen of Kecskemét voiced a common complaint that "the Germans do not leave any udder of the cow unmilked."[18] In 1698, for example, the court set the annual tax in Hungary at four million forints, twice the annual tax levied from 1694 to 1697. Without obtaining the assent of the Hungarian estates, Leopold levied the tax and demanded that the counties collect the payment in cash, not in kind as had been the former policy. This stipulation proved a particular hardship for the serfs, on whom the tax burden already fell heaviest and most disproportionately. This 1698 tax illustrates the Habsburg strategy of lessening the drain from the imperial treasury by extending the base of taxation to include not only the serfs but also the burghers and nobles. It signaled a decisive victory for the crown over the nobility because the basic unit of taxation was no longer the villein tenure but the manor. Second, though the nobles paid only a small sum, they were forced to pay a tax, an abrogation of yet another traditional liberty: exemption from taxation. The conquered were also forced to pay the portion, a tax collected in kind to support the army. An equally unpopular and newly imposed tax was the turnover, levied on the sale of beer, wine, brandy, meat, and various animals in towns, boroughs, markets, and fairs. Leopold's advisers predicted that this tax would prove a lucrative source of revenue because of the importance of the agricultural sector of the economy and because it was designed to fall heaviest on those who produced and traded in commodities, not only the serfs but the nobles as well. Many of the nobles in fact derived most of their income from trading and objected vehemently to this new impost, which together with the discriminatory tariffs levied on Hungarian products imported into the hereditary countries made their products more expensive and therefore less competitive.

The introduction of monopolies and the prohibition of certain exports further disrupted trade patterns. For example, Leopold granted the Orientalische Compagnie the monopoly on all trade with the Turks and on the sale of cattle to Vienna and Silesia. The crown also forbade the exportation of cattle to Venice and Poland, arguing that they were needed to feed the army, and restricted the trade in wine. The Habsburgs also granted their chief banker, Samuel Oppenheimer, the preemption to trade in corn throughout the kingdom. But the most indispensable item, salt, was made the exclusive and lucrative monopoly of the state in 1699. By establishing monopolies the government restricted the growth of key industries, such as paper, and enriched the court aristocracy. The Habsburgs had thus expropriated both foreign and home markets, excluding certain groups from trade and causing a marked and predictable increase in prices. The nobility, in particular, resented the restrictions on trade, for they considered free trade a fundamental liberty. Pragmatically, the nobles opposed such practices because many of them derived most of their income from trading in wine, salt, honey, and meat. The great-grandfather of Thököly, a famous seventeenth-century Hungarian aristocrat, for example, had accumulated a large fortune by dealing in cattle. But it was the lower classes who suffered the most. As a consequence of these and other disastrous policies, bandits, fugitive serfs, and former soldiers roamed the countryside; they fled the excessive taxation, the plundering armies, and the threat of conscription, sometimes going into exile in Poland, Silesia, and the Turkish lands. Desperate peasants even attempted to sell their children to the Turks for money. Predictably the abandonment of villein allotments intensified the labor shortage. The number of *cottars* (part owners) increased and that of owners decreased, for *cottars* paid far less in taxes. At the onset of the eighteenth century landless peasants and *cottars* were unknown in many parts of Hungary, but by 1828 they made up about 47.2 percent of the peasant population and by 1848 nearly 66.6 percent. In both Hungary and Transylvania lords bought, sold, and even gave away landless serfs. The last known transaction took place in Hungary in 1773, in Transylvania in the 1780s.[19] Exemplative of the dissatisfaction was Tamas Esze, one of the early leaders of the revolt. Esze, a serf who had turned to smuggling salt for his livelihood, had urged Rákóczi to "liberate salt and drive out the portion."[20] His plight resembled that of many others who considered themselves "exiles in their own country."[21]

Leopold had only succeeded in deepening this estrangement by openly favoring Catholics in the allocating of land and in the granting of imperial patents, monopolies, and licenses. Only Catholics, Leopold stipulated, had the right to enter guilds, live in cities, and obtain conquered territory. Protestants were legally barred from office until the mid-eighteenth century. Leopold's policies contrasted sharply with those of the Turks, who had adopted a policy of indifference rather than toleration toward the various Christian sects. Even though the special courts that enforced the policies of the Jesuits and the Counter-Reformation no longer existed in 1703, discrimination against Protestants continued. The closing of yet another Protestant school, the establishment of yet another Jesuit foundation only fueled Hungarian resentment. As king, Leopold had sworn to honor the traditional Hungarian liberties including that of religion. As ruler of a multiconfessional state, he had vowed to respect the rights not only of Catholics but Calvinists and Lutherans, as well as the numerically less significant groups. He had not kept his word.[22] In contrast, Rákóczi, himself a Catholic, offered liberty of conscience for all faiths and encouraged the different confessions to establish their own schools.

The crown's policies had only served to mobilize support for Rákóczi and his cause from all strata in Hungarian society—social, religious, and ethnic. Although the serfs numerically dominated the insurrectionist army, other groups such as discharged veterans, burghers, nobles, and even former Habsburg officers such as Counts Antal Esterházy and Simon Forgách fought as well. The insurgent army also included armed bands of soldiers, serfs, and outcasts who roamed throughout and terrorized the countryside. Their warlike and often barbarous tactics, and especially their mastery of unconventional warfare, made them invaluable but often resistant to discipline. To an initial motley band of some six hundred ill-clad, badly equipped peasants, Rákóczi added approximately eight hundred Polish mercenaries and Ukrainian peasants from his estates in the Carpathians. This small band mushroomed to an effective fighting force of some seventy thousand and included Ruthenians, Romanians, and Slovaks[23] as well as Hungarians, Germans, and Ukrainians. In order to encourage enrollment in the army, Rákóczi exempted armed serfs and their families from seigneurial dues. The Patent of Szerencs further confirmed their exemption from levies or taxes. In contrast, the Habsburgs released the serfs who enrolled only from billeting, not from their seigneurial obligations. Serfs not in the army, Rákóczi insisted, must still fulfill their obligations to their lord and to the state (Patent of Vetes, 28 August 1703). For those serfs who fought for the entire war he promised personal freedom. Only later in the struggle did Rákóczi establish a type of draft, assigning quotas to the different counties.[24]

In spite of the diverse composition of the fighting force, Rákóczi hoped to create a well-disciplined regular army and wage conventional warfare. Unfortunately, he lost all of the six large-scale pitched battles that he fought. The engagement near Trencsén in August 1708 proved particularly disastrous, for it undermined the Hungarians' will to resist. The rebels did achieve some success; in 1703 they took Debrecen, Nagy Szombat, and Pozsony, and eventually they seized most of the land east of the Danube. By 1704 the rebels had even raided the suburbs around Vienna, alarming the populace, who feared that the Hungarians might seize the capital. But the defeats in the latter stages of the war counterbalanced the victories and destroyed morale. Ineffective leadership and untrained and badly disciplined troops, as well as the officers' and Rákóczi's lack of professional military training, doomed these efforts. Most of Rákóczi's followers had no previous military experience; those who did, the *hajdu* and Thököly veterans, were trained in unconventional guerrilla warfare. Hungarian forces had traditionally excelled in unconventional warfare, mobile warfare, the use of light cavalry, and the avoidance of pitched battle. Their success lay in raiding enemy supply lines and enemy territory, seizing fortresses through attrition, and living off the country. The mastery of light-troop tactics in particular resulted directly from the needs of defending the frontier. Through such tactics the Hungarians were able to prevent the complete absorption of their country into the Habsburg empire. By 1703 the Hungarians had employed light cavalry to occupy the land, to raid enemy supplies and supply lines, and to ravage the border areas. The *kuruc* leaders consciously strove to destroy the enemy by attrition, by adopting scorched-earth tactics, burning villages and supplies and devastating the countryside. Such a policy inevitably and fatally destroyed the scanty resources and dramatically increased the war-weariness of the populace.[25] Rákóczi, though a statesman and a diplomat, was not a soldier. He had tried unsuccessfully to transform his forces into a regular army.

His forces suffered from not only tactical but also logistical inferiority. Supplying the soldiers with arms and ammunition proved an almost insuperable problem. Because of limited assistance from abroad, Rákóczi had to equip the army chiefly at his own expense and to expropriate local taxes, such as the tithe, to obtain badly needed funds. Motivated in part by necessity and in part by mercantilistic convictions, Rákóczi established monopolies for several goods and state control of the mineral and salt mines. He also drastically increased taxes, demanding even more than the Habsburgs had in the 1690s. Such tactics fueled the accusation that Rákóczi was more tyrannical than the emperor and increased the discontent. Simon Forgách and others, who opposed Rákóczi's absolutist government, advocated instead a government that would give unlimited power to the nobility.[26] Rákóczi, however, had to adopt such expedients, for the Hungarians were desperately short of funds. This shortage hamstrung all efforts and forced the insurgents to adopt more creative strategies such as bartering wine, copper, and cattle for supplies. External events such as the Great Northern War compounded the problem by making the importation of firearms and ammunition from the traditional source, Poland, virtually impossible. Because he could not get supplies from abroad, Rákóczi set up his own factories at Besztercebánya, Kassa, and Gömör and established magazines at Ersekújvar, Kassa, and Munkács. In spite of the noteworthy efforts of war commissars such as Ferenc Lónyai and Pál Lányi, hunger caused soldiers to mutiny and shortages caused maneuvers to fail. A fully armed cavalryman was a rarity. Pay too proved a problem. At the outset soldiers were paid in copper coinage, but by 1708 the government had so depreciated the currency that soldiers received in effect only half pay. Toward the end of the war many soldiers even declined to collect their pay in order to relieve the burdens of the beleaguered insurgent government. In view of the difficulties the Hungarians faced, the *kuruc* achievements were remarkable.[27]

Rákóczi also strove to legitimize the movement by convoking assemblies at Szécsény (9 September 1705) and Ónod (May 1707). At Szécsény delegates from the towns, *komitats* (administrative units around the castles), the nobility, and the church urged the reinstatement of Hungarian liberties and the recognition of Transylvania as a sovereign entity, refused to recognize the new Habsburg emperor Joseph I as king of Hungary, and established a council to regulate foreign and economic affairs. At Ónod the assembly met to discuss the worsening economic situation, particularly the depreciation of the copper currency, and the sensitive problem of formally dethroning the Habsburgs. The representatives for Turóc opposed the introduction of a general tax and urged instead renewal of negotiations with the Habsburgs. This suggestion enraged Bercsényi, who slew one of the delegates in full view of the assembly and had the other executed the next day. The assembly subsequently agreed to levy a general tax, dethroned the Habsburgs, and elected Rákóczi prince of Transylvania. Rákóczi had attained this success at great cost; Bercsényi's treatment of the dissenting representatives helped to alienate many of his followers.[28]

Just as Rákóczi sought support at home, so too did he seek

support abroad. Rákóczi realized that he also needed the military, financial, and diplomatic support of foreign powers in order to succeed. His chances for success hinged on his ability to transform a small localized struggle into an international one, to make the Hungarian insurrection a European affair.[29] He turned to Leopold's enemies, France, Bavaria, and the Turks, and to neutrals such as Augustus II of Poland, Charles XII of Sweden, and Peter I of Russia. He even appealed, and in part successfully, to Leopold's allies, England, the United Provinces, and Brandenburg-Prussia.

Comparatively, Rákóczi had more success with France. Louis XIV subsidized the insurrection with approximately fifty thousand livres per month until 1708, but this covered the pay of only two thousand soldiers out of a total army of seventy thousand. Louis XIV also encouraged the Turks to ally with the Hungarians, but he did little else. In 1703 Louis could well have reiterated the remarks he had made in the 1670s to his minister in Poland: "In according rewards to the Hungarian chiefs it is my intention to drive them forward on a path which they have voluntarily entered and which they are no more free to leave. It is not my intention to accord to them such means that they could thereby sustain their troops." He wanted, he said, "to excite anxiety in Vienna" but not to "entertain by great expense a war so far away and so little regular as those based on popular revolt generally are."[30] He certainly tried to dissuade Rákóczi from settling with or even negotiating with the Habsburgs, for the insurgency did give France more leverage in the war. In 1704, for example, the *kuruc* advance into Styria and toward Vienna coincided with the French thrust toward Passau. To the east in Poland, Russia, and Sweden, Rákóczi had less success; Peter, Charles, and Augustus, mired in the ongoing Northern War (1700–1721), would not alienate the Habsburgs, who might be provoked to intervene in that conflict.[31]

With Leopold's allies, paradoxically, Rákóczi was more successful, for through them pressure was exerted on Leopold and later Joseph to negotiate with the insurgents. The Maritime Powers had some leverage in Vienna because the Austrians were dependent on them for both military and financial assistance. They were effective too because they presented a united front to the Austrians; they acted in concert, often submitting joint memorials. England, the dominant partner in the alliance, tended to express the views of both while the Dutch merely echoed English concerns. But at times the Dutch did put pressure on the English to act. It was the States General who argued as early as 1704 that a special commission of Charles Spencer, earl of Sunderland (1643–1722), and Count Adolf Hendrik Rechteren, Baron D'Almelo (1658–1731), be sent to Vienna to buttress the efforts of their representatives George Stepney (1663–1707) and Jacob Jan Hamel-Bruynincx (1662–1738). And it was the States General in 1707 and 1709 who urged John Churchill, duke of Marlborough, the allied commander, to press the emperor to accept Anglo-Dutch mediation yet again.[32]

But why did the English and Dutch urge their ally to negotiate with the insurgents? As Protestant states and constitutional governments, England and the United Provinces felt a special kinship with the Hungarians, whom they saw struggling against popery and despotism. Rákóczi frequently appealed to the so-called Evangelical alliance among Protestant states and depicted himself as a champion not of toleration but of Protestantism. He unhesitatingly exploited the religious issue, arguing as late as 1709 in a letter to Marlborough, the allied commander, that the Protestant religion would be extirpated in Hungary unless a settlement was reached with the emperor before the conclusion of a general peace.[33] Still later Rákóczi would attempt to have the Hungarian issue discussed at Utrecht, two years after the settlement at Szatmár. He had underplayed the multiconfessional nature of Hungary and won over both the English and the Dutch representatives stationed in Vienna. They in turn supported the views of persuasive publicists like Henry St. John, Viscount Bolingbroke, that "a spirit of bigotry, tyranny, and avarice" had caused the troubles in Hungary.[34] Hamel-Bruynincx importuned the States General to act, arguing that never again would there be "such a good opportunity to reestablish Protestant rights and privileges."[35] Throughout the insurrection the Maritime Powers' and Prussia's[36] sympathies remained with the Hungarians, whom they saw "fighting only to protect their religion and liberty."[37]

The Maritime Powers were also trying to safeguard the imperial war effort. They feared that the Habsburg withdrawal of troops from the Rhine to Hungary would only prolong the war with

France.[38] Imperial resources, they argued, were already overtaxed. The emperor could not carry on a war in Italy, the Rhine, and Hungary simultaneously; he did not even fulfill his quota of troops—and those he did supply were so poorly equipped that the imperial commander, Prince Eugene of Savoy, threatened to resign on more than one occasion.[39] Financially, Austria was on the brink of bankruptcy. The insurgents' raids on the empire had further decreased trade and reduced the imperial tax yields. The Habsburgs had lost the income not only from taxes, customs, and the salt monopoly but also from the Hungarian copper and Transylvanian mercury mines.[40] Lastly, the Maritime Powers feared that the Turks might, at French instigation, launch yet another conflict with their old enemy, Austria.[41]

Although the English and the Dutch urged the Habsburgs to negotiate, neither Leopold nor Joseph intended to honor Hungarian constitutionalist demands; they negotiated with the insurrectionists only in order to appease their allies and to gain time for a military solution.[42] The Habsburgs did negotiate with the Hungarians intermittently from the spring of 1704 to the summer of 1706. Truces were periodically concluded, commissioners empowered to treat. But neither Leopold nor Joseph would agree to sanction a foreign guarantee of the agreement, to abolish the hereditary succession, or to recognize Rákóczi as prince of Transylvania. In spite of Habsburg intransigence, Rákóczi continued to urge both the English and the Dutch to offer their mediation yet again in 1706, 1707, 1709, 1710, and 1711.[43] He even went so far as to write Queen Anne personally, urging her intercession for his "oppressed" people.[44] Rákóczi also dispatched his envoys, men like Domokos Brenner and János Klement, to the peace conferences at Gertruydenberg and Utrecht to argue his case.[45] Taking advantage of both the English and Dutch empathy with the Hungarian Protestants, Rákóczi sent representatives from the Hungarian churches directly to the Protestant churches abroad in order to sway the English, Dutch, and Prussian governments. But in spite of all this pressure, both direct and indirect, by Rákóczi and through his agents, Rákóczi did not succeed in making the Hungarian insurrection a European affair. The Habsburgs had refused even to discuss the situation in Hungary with the allies after 1706. They had deliberately kept the allies uninformed about the course of the negotiations with the insurrectionists—and so it remained. After the failure of the peace negotiations in 1706 and particularly after the conclusion of the settlement at Szatmár in 1711, allied strategic concerns were not involved in Hungary. Rákóczi's hopes of persuading the allies to intervene were completely unrealistic. He deluded himself in thinking that they would or could do anything about Hungary, particularly after 1711.[46] Rákóczi then had tried but failed to merge a local national war into the ongoing international conflict in the West. The Habsburgs never deviated from their view that the Hungarian war had nothing to do with the War of the Spanish Succession. Rákóczi had continued to hope that the international situation would change and that Hungary would gain from it. The international situation did change, but not for the better, at least not for the Hungarians. Hungary did not become an international concern, but the Hungarians undoubtedly had benefited from the Habsburg commitment to the War of the Spanish Succession. By 1711 the Viennese court, concerned about the upcoming general peace, was anxious to conciliate the Hungarians, end the war, and prevent future unrest. At all costs they sought to avoid international mediation, to avoid dealing with Hungary as a state in its own right.[47]

Many insurgents, too, advocated peace, for the situation in Hungary was desperate, particularly for the peasants. The scorched-earch tactics of the soldiers meant that homes and property were destroyed. Furthermore, the necessity of supplying the armed forces forced the insurgents to depreciate the currency, to levy even higher taxes, and to confiscate scarce resources. Hungary had lost 410,000 in the plague epidemic and another 85,000 in battle; this meant that a much smaller populace had to meet the fiscal demands of a society at war.[48] One of the very reasons for Rákóczi's success, his ability to garner support from both the nobility and the lower classes, generated internal contradictions, which helped to doom the insurrection. The nobles, for example, assumed leadership over what had once been a popular movement. As more nobles, such as Sándor Károlyi, pledged themselves to Rákóczi, the tone of the movement changed. By late 1705 only one member of the lower classes, János Bottyán, served as a general; the other twenty-five were from the nobility. In the later years of the war, popular support for Rákóczi's cause eroded, partially because of his inability to keep his commitments to the serfs. Bercsényi himself realized this in 1707 when he commented that they had "lost the love of the common people."[49] In 1703, Rákóczi had promised personal freedom to those serfs who fought and to their descendants. The landowners who joined the insurrection had forced Rákóczi to go back on his word. Rákóczi's decision in 1708 to push through a law ensuring freedom for those who were still fighting came too late to counter the growing disaffection. The insoluble economic problems that the insurgents faced, the war-weariness of the population, and the shrinking economic resources made a settlement unavoidable. Famine and disease coupled with the military defeats, particularly the loss at Trencsén (August 1708) and the capitulation of the fort of Érsekújvár (September 1710), gave the Hungarians little option. Many realized, too, that once the war in the West was over the Habsburgs could and would concentrate more of their forces in Hungary. Many of the nobility, such as Sándor Károlyi, realized the necessity of reaching a settlement with the Habsburgs. Deputed to head the army in the absence of Rákóczi and Bercsényi, who had gone to Poland to garner support from the tsar, Károlyi opened talks with János Pálffy, commander of the Habsburg forces. When the Habsburgs offered amnesty and the return of *kuruc* property, Károlyi accepted and disbanded the army, now a mere 12,000, at Szatmár (May 1711).

The subsequent Treaty of Szatmár (30 April 1711) represented a compromise between the Habsburgs and the Hungarian estates. Ironically, the war that had begun as a popular uprising ended with a settlement that did not even mention the main protagonists, the serfs. The peace secured not the rights of the serfs but those of the landowners. It reestablished Hungarian constitutional self-government and guaranteed the Hungarian basic liberties including freedom of conscience for the Protestants. The Habsburgs agreed to respect the constitutional privileges as formulated in 1687, granted amnesty for those who fought in the war, restored confiscated estates, and guaranteed the privileges of the warrior estate. The general assemblies met again on a regular basis, and the *komitats* regained their former rights. In turn the Hungarians acknowledged the hereditary succession of the Habsburg dynasty in the male line. This settlement marked a retreat from earlier insurgent demands, for the Hungarians did not insist upon the independence of Transylvania or a foreign guarantee of the agreement. Determined to prevent the recurrence of yet another uprising, the Habsburgs moved the Hungarian chancellery to Vienna and retained control of the Hungary army, insisting that at least half be non-Hungarian. Whether Szatmár really represented a victory for the Habsburgs or a compromise,[50] it nonetheless proved successful, for it marked the onset of a period of reconstruction and repopulation.

Not all, however, accepted the settlement. Rákóczi placed no faith in what he termed the emperor's "specious promises"[51] and fled abroad, first to Poland, then to France, and later to the Ottoman Empire. There he ultimately died—an exile to the end, still futilely hoping to convince the Great Powers to intervene for him at the subsequent general peace conferences.

NOTES

1. Orest Subtelny, *Domination of Eastern Europe: Native Nobilities and Foreign Absolutism 1500-1715* (Montreal, 1986), pp. 53-59.

2. For Rákóczi's life consult Béla Köpeczi, Lajos Hopp, and Ágnes Várkonyi, eds., *Rákóczi-Tanulmányok* (Budapest, 1980); *Archivum Rákóczianum*, 14 vols. (Budapest, 1873-1889, 1935, 1955-1961); Emile Horn, *François Rákóczy II, Prince de Transylvanie* (Paris, 1906), pp. 1-101; François Rákóczy II, *Testament politique et moral* (The Hague, 1751), pp. 1-72; François Rákóczy II, *Histoire* (Cassovie, 1707), pp. 1-77; Albert Lefaivre, *Les Magyars pendant le domination ottomane en Hongrie, 1526-1721* (Paris, 1902), p. 306; Onno Klopp, *Der Fall des Hauses Stuart* (Vienna, 1879) 10:291-292; George Michel de Boislisle, ed., *Mémoires de Saint-Simon* (Paris, 1928), 5:260.

3. Subtelny, *Domination of Eastern Europe*, p. 147.

4. P. Zs. Pach, "Le Probléme du rassemblement des forces nationales pendant la guerre d'indépendance de François II Rákóczi," *Acta Historica* 3 (1956):97; Joseph Joubert, *François Rákóczy II, Prince de Transylvania* (Angiers, 1907), p. 11; Redlich, *Österreich*, pp. 155-161; refer to Fritz Posch, *Flammende Grenze: Die Steiermark in den Kuruzzensturmen* (Vienna, 1968); François Rákóczy II, *Histoire de revolution de Hongrie avec les mémoires* (The Hague, 1739), pp. 80-306; *Feldzüge des Prinzen Eugen von Savoyen* (Vienna, 1876), 3:83-86; London, Public Record Office, State Papers Germany, 105/71, 365-370, 371-372, 393-398; hereafter cited as P.R.O., S.P. Germany; Gy. Rázsó, "La Situation militaire générale

et la guerre d'indépendance de Rákóczi," *Acta Historica Academiae Scientiarum Hungaricae* 22 (1976); B. Köpeczi, "La Guerre d'indépendance hongroise au début du XVIII siècle et l'Europe," *Acta Historica* 22 (1976):331–341.

5. Ágnes Várkonyi, "Rákóczi's War of Independence and the Peasantry," *War and Society in Eastern Central Europe*, vol. 3, *From Hunyadi to Rákóczi: War and Society in Late Medieval and Early Modern Hungary*, edited by Béla K. Király and János M. Bak (New York, 1982), p. 373.

6. Subtelny, *Domination of Eastern Europe*, p. 147.

7. Béla K. Király, "War and Society in Western and East Central Europe in the Pre-Revolutionary Eighteenth Century," *War and Society in Eastern Central Europe*, vol. 2, *East Central European Society and War in the Pre-Revolutionary Eighteenth Century*, edited by Gunther E. Rothenberg, Béla K. Király, and Peter F. Sugar (New York, 1982), p. 13.

8. Pach, "Le Problème du rassemblement," p. 99.

9. Subtelny, *Domination of Eastern Europe*, p. 105.

10. Ibid., p. 79.

11. John P. Spielman, *Leopold I of Austria* (New Brunswick, N. J., 1977), p. 140. Also refer to Ágnes Várkonyi, "Repopulation and the System of Cultivation in Hungary after the Expulsion of the Turks," *Acta Historica* 16 (1970):151–169.

12. Kurt Wessely, "The Development of the Hungarian Military Frontier until the Middle of the Eighteenth Century," *Austrian History Yearbook* 9–10 (1973–1974):55–63.

13. Ibid., p. 63.

14. Géza Perjés, "Reflections on the Strategic Decisions of Ferenc II Rákóczi's War of Independence," in *From Hunyadi to Rákóczi*, pp. 417, 406.

15. Ferenc Rákóczi, II, *Mémoires du Prince François II Rakoczi sur la guerre de Hongrie depuis 1703 jusqu'a sa fin* (Budapest, 1978) pp. 16, 20, 54.

16. P. G. M. Dickson and John Sperling, "War Finance 1689–1714," *New Cambridge Modern History*, edited by J. S. Bromley (Cambridge, 1970), 6:305–313; Franz von Mensi, *Die Finanzen Oesterreichs von 1701 bis 1740* (Vienna, 1890); and Jean Berenger, *Finances et absolutisme autrichien dans la seconde moitié du XVII siècle* (Paris, 1975), passim.

17. P. Zs. Pach, "The Diminishing Share of East-Central Europe in the 17th Century International Trade," *Acta Historica* 16 (1970):289–306, and "The Shifting of International Trade Routes in the 15th–17th Centuries," *Acta Historica* 14(1968):287–321.

18. Ágnes Várkonyi, "Habsburg Absolutism and Serfdom in Hungary at the Turn of the 17th and 18th Centuries," *Nouvelle études historiques*

1 (1965): 385; also refer to Ágnes Várkonyi, "Évolution sociale et autonomie de l'État (L'Absolutisme des Habsbourg et l'indépendance de la Hongrie)," *Acta Historica* 22 (1976): 349–350.

19. Blum, *The End of the Old Order*, pp. 106, 42.

20. Várkonyi, "Habsburg Absolutism," p. 386.

21. Várkonyi, "Rákóczi's War and the Peasantry," p. 371. Also see Várkonyi, "Évolution sociale," pp. 343–365; and Charles Eszlary, "La Situation des serfs en Hongrie de 1514 à 1848," *Revue d'histoire économique et sociale* 38 (1961):385–417.

22. Mihaly Bucsay, *Der Protestantismus in Ungarn, 1521–1978*, (Vienna, 1977).

23. Ágnes Várkonyi, "Politique envers les serfs et développement culturel dans l'ètat de Rákóczi," *Acta Historica* 27 (1981):57–58.

24. Király, "War and Society"; Várkonyi, "Rákóczi's War and the Peasantry"; and Pach, "Le Problème du rassemblement," pp. 100–107.

25. Perjés, "Reflections on the Strategic Decisions of Ferenc II Rákóczi's War of Independence."

26. Várkonyi, "Évolution sociale," pp. 358–360.

27. Király, "War and Society"; Géza Perjés, "Reflections on the Strategic Decisions of Ferenc II Rákóczi's War of Independence"; and Gusztav Heckenast, "Equipment and Supply of Ferenc II Rákóczi's Army"; *From Hunyadi to Rákóczi*, pp. 393–419 and 421–431; Rázsó, "La Situation militaire generale"; and Pach, "Le Problème du rassemblement," pp. 95–113.

28. Subtelny, *Domination of Eastern Europe*, pp. 151–153.

29. Rázsó, "La Situation militaire."

30. Quoted in Ladislas Hengelmüller, *Hungary's Fight for National Existence* (London, 1913), p. 45.

31. Béla Köpeczi, *La France et la Hongrie au début de XVIII siècle* (Budapest, 1971), Kalman Benda, "The Rákóczi War of Independence and the European Powers," Béla Köpeczi, "The Hungarian Wars of Independence of the Seventeenth and Eighteenth in their European Context," and Peter Pastor, "Hungarian-Russian Relations during the Rákóczi War of Independence," in *From Hunyadi to Rákóczi*, 433–444, 445–454, and 467–492; Onno Klopp, *Der Fall des Hauses Stuart* (Vienna, 1879) 10:291; Arsène Legrelle, *La diplomatie française et la succession d'Espagne* (Paris, 1892) 5:120–129; Jean Baptiste Colbert, marquis de Torcy, *Mémoires* (The Hague, 1757) 1:221–222.

32. Linda and Marsha Frey, "The Rákóczi Insurrection and the Disruption of the Grand Alliance," *Canadian American Review of Hungarian Studies* 5 (Fall 1978): 17–29; "Rákóczi and the Maritime Powers: An Uncertain Friendship," in *From Hunyadi to Rákóczi*, pp. 455–466; and

"II. Rákóczi Ferenc és a tengeri hatalmak," *Történelmi Szemle* no. 4 (June 1981), pp. 663–674; John Hattendorf, "The Rákóczi Insurrection in English War Policy, 1703–1711," *Canadian-American Review of Hungarian Studies* 7 (Fall 1980); pp. 91–102.

33. B.M., Blenheim Papers, British Diplomatic Correspondence, M36, Raby to Marlborough, Berlin?, 22 January 1709.

34. Henry St. John, Viscount Bolingbroke, *Works* (London, 1754) 2:459.

35. Algemeen Rijksarchief, Archief, Staten Generaal 6587, Hamel-Bruynincx Report of 5 February 1704, hereafter cited as Alg. Rijks.

36. Kálmán Benda, "Le Projet d'alliance hungaro-suedo-prussienne de 1704," *Études historiques* 1 (1960):669–694; Budapest, Országos Levéltár, Rákóczi Asprement 9.15, vol. 114, Prussia fols. 15–19, Frederick to Rákóczi; vol. 164, fols. 28–31, Saint Julien, 15 October 1709; vol. 164, fols. 28–31 Rákóczi memoire to deputies of Protestant church; ZSTA, Auswärtige Beziehungen, Rep 11, Ungarn, Nr. 278 and 279, passim.

37. British Museum, Additional Manuscripts, B.M., Add. Mss. 31, 132, fol. 164, Raby to Hill, Berlin 10 May 1704, hereafter cited as B.M.

38. B.M., Add. Mss. 28, 915, fols. 99–101, Ellis to Stanhope, 21 December 1703; Add. Mss. 37, 351, fols. 217–218, Hedges to Whitworth, 21 December 1703 and in P.R.O., S.P. Germany, 105/71/51; B. M., Add. Mss. 31, 132, fol. 37, Raby's Letter of 26 January 1704, Berlin and fol. 39, Raby to Hill, Berlin, 26 January 1704; Alg. Rijks., Report of 19 February 1704.

39. B.M., Add. Mss. 9096, fol. 180, Halifax to Marlborough, The Hague, 18 August 1706, Add. Mss. 7059, fols. 180–182, Stepney to Harley, Vienna, Add. Mss. 37, 351, fol. 369, Whitworth to Hedges, Vienna, 16 January 1704, B.M. Blenheim Papers, M38, Stepney Papers, Stepney to Hedges, Vienna, 4 April 1703, Haus- Hof- und Staatsarchiv, England Kart, 37, Bericht (report) Wratislaw to Leopold, 5 January 1703, hereafter cited as HHSA.

40. B.M., Add. Mss. 37, 353, fols. 350–351, Whitworth to Hedges, Vienna, 9 January 1704; Klopp, *Der Fall des Hauses Stuart*, 11:46–48; Franz Mensi, *Die Finanzen Österreichs von 1701 bis 1740* (Vienna: Hof-Verlags- und Universität-Buchhandlung, 1890); Max Grunwald, *Samuel Oppenheimer und sein Kreis: Ein Kapitel aus der Finanzgeschichte Österreichs* (Vienna, 1913).

41. B.M., Add. Mss. 37, 352 and in P.R.O., S.P. Germany, 80/21, Sutton to Whitworth, Pera of Constantinople, 7 November 1703; P.R.O., S.P. 80/22, Sutton to Whitworth, Pera of Constantinople, 27 October 1703; B.M., Add. Mss. 28, 914, fol. 237, Stepney to Ellis, 24 July 1703 and 4 August 1703; Add. Mss. 36, 351, fol. 92, Whitworth to Hedges, 25 No-

vember 1703; B.M. Add. Mss. 37, 156, fols. 214–217, Refléxions sur les Affaires d'Hongrie, 5 October 1704; Alg. Rjks., Arch. Staten Generaal 6587, Hamel-Bruynincx to States Generaal, 30 August 1704; P.R.O., S.P. Germany, 80/32/200, Sutton to Stepney, Pera of Constantinople, 2 March 1704, B.M., Add. Mss., 21, 551, fol. 23, Sutton to Stepney, Pera of Constantinople, 26 March 1704. Also refer to Akdes Nimet Kurat, *The Despatches of Sir Robert Sutton, Ambassador to Constantinople (1710–1714)* (London: Offices of the Royal Historical Society, 1953). Rákóczi too feared Turkish intentions and worried, as he told Des Alleurs, about the Turkish "pretensions" to the lands he had seized. See B.M. Blenheim Papers, Sunderland Papers, S2, "Journal of the Ministers of England and the United Provinces for the Hungarian Mediation" (27 August to 4 November 1705). Particularly see inclusions therein of the Memoir of Des Alleurs to Rákóczi and Rákóczi's response of 18 March 1705 and Reflections of Des Alleurs on the Present State of Affairs in Hungary regarding the Ottoman Porte, 1 April 1705.

42. For Joseph's attitude see Charles Ingrao, *In Quest and Crisis: Emperor Joseph I and the Habsburg Monarchy* (West Lafayette, Ind., 1979), pp. 123–160.

43. P.R.O., S.P. 90/5, Rákóczi to Anne, 1710, fol. 490, Rákóczi to States General, 30 August 1710, fol. 476; Merseburg, Zentrales Staatsarchiv, Rep. 11, Ungarn 279, Spanheim Report of 24 February 1709/4 March 1710, Rákóczi to States General, 20 December 1706, fol. 97, Rákóczi to Marlborough, 20 October 1709, fol. 143.

44. P.R.O., S.P. 90/5, Rákóczi to Anne, 1710, fol. 490.

45. Á. R. Várkonyi, " 'Ad pacem universalem': The International Antecedents of the Peace of Szatmár," *Études historiques hongroises* 1 (1980):305–337.

46. Linda and Marsha Frey, "Insurgency during the War of the Spanish Succession: The Rákóczi Revolt," *American Historical Association Proceedings*, 1982.

47. Várkonyi, " 'Ad pacem universalem.' "

48. Béla K. Király, *Hungary in the Late Eighteenth Century: The Decline of Enlightened Despotism* (New York, 1969), p. 5; and Várkonyi, "Politique envers les serfs," pp. 49–50.

49. Subtelny, *Domination of Eastern Europe*, p. 152.

50. Ibid., pp. 153–156.

51. Rákóczi, *Mémoires*, p. 194. Also see Domokos Brenner, *Histoire des révolutions de Hongrie* (The Hague, 1739).

4

Spain

In Spain revolt also threatened to undermine the state, to weaken the hold that Philip V had on his new dominions. Only a short time after Philip became king, he faced civil war; large areas of the kingdom of Aragon openly acclaimed his rival, Archduke Charles of Austria, Charles III. Only the Castilians remained unswervingly loyal to Philip. The lands that awaited Philip on 28 January 1701 were a far cry from the Spain of Philip II and Philip V's own beloved France. Spain was not the moribund shell of a once vital empire, as contemporaries and subsequent historians have all too often—and graphically—depicted it. Although it was a country "both bleeding and impoverished,"[1] it was also a country recovering both economically and demographically. Bourbon apologists have distorted and magnified the deterioration of Spain in the late seventeenth century, in part to highlight the achievements of the new dynasty. Foreigners influenced by the "Black Legend" have also sought to denigrate Spain, attributing her decline to monarchical absolutism, rigid Catholicism, and the "inherent" cruelty and treachery of the Spanish. Today Spain continues to personify "far beyond historical realities the evils of the Roman Catholic state church, the barbarities of the New World conquest, and a generalized moral-physical-intellectual inferiority."[2] But even seventeenth-century Spaniards, disillusioned with the government and the monarchy, thought Spain's decline was irreversible and bemoaned the fate of their land under Philip's Habsburg predecessor, Charles II.

Known to history as Charles the Bewitched, Charles was the product of excessive inbreeding. As a sixth-generation Habsburg, he possessed all of the family traits: pale, light eyes; the large, pendulous so-called Habsburg jaw, which jutted out so far that his teeth did not meet and forced him to swallow his food whole; a long, narrow forehead; a large chin; and acrocephaly, an endocrine dysfunction that caused physical deformity. Short of stature, with a huge, balding forehead, Charles tottered rather than walked. Epileptic fits, convulsions, fainting spells, ulcers, and congenital syphilis, a direct result of his father's promiscuity, plagued Charles during his short life. Nervous, weak-minded, melancholic, and conscience-ridden like his predecessors, he—and many others—believed that the devil possessed him; thus the sobriquet Charles the Bewitched. Charles was clearly unfit to rule, but rule he did, surprising Europe by surviving for thirty-nine years. His mother, his half-brother, and a succession of strong ministers dominated him. Intense jockeying for power over the question of Charles's heir darkened his last years. The court was rent between two factions; one group supported Charles of Austria, the other Philip of France. Balancing his hatred of the French against his desire to pass his kingdoms on undivided to his successor, Charles willed his lands in entirety to Philip of Anjou. Shortly thereafter Charles died, and predictably war over the succession erupted. During the War of the Spanish Succession (1702–1714) France allied with Spain, Bavaria, and Cologne against Austria, the Holy Roman Empire, England, the United Provinces, Prussia, Savoy, and Portugal. Spain faced not only an international conflict but a civil war as well, for part of Spain supported Philip and part supported Charles. The ultimate result of the war was the division of the Spanish lands, the outcome that Charles had labored so hard and so futilely to avoid. During Charles's later years the question of an heir obsessed him and the court. The real power in Spain resided with the church and the aristocracy, not the king. The nepotism, corruption, favoritism, and pluralism; the superfluity of offices; and the monopolization of the administration by a closed circle paint a gray picture of Charles II's government. The vacuum at the core of government encouraged federalism and decentralization; more and more power, both political and economic, gravitated to the provinces, which had benefited from the weak government of the last Habsburg.

Philip's "splendid gift" was a congeries of different jurisdictions, each with its own laws, governments, and coinage. Though the empire centered on Castile, the laws and taxes of Castile pertained only in Castile. Ever since the crowns of Aragon and Castile had been united by Ferdinand and Isabella in the fifteenth century, the two lands had retained their own laws and liberties, or *fueros*. Castilian authority did not extend to the other provinces of Biscay, Guipuzcoa, or Alava, and it was even more restricted in the Italian lands, Sicily, Naples, and Milan. But Castilians did dominate both old and new Spain, and they were bitterly resented in the lands of the crown of Aragon, which included the kingdoms of Valencia and Aragon, the principality of Catalonia, Sardinia, and the Balearic Islands. The gulf between Castile and Aragon yawned wide, both historically and politically. The Aragonese, for example, prided themselves on their tradition of liberty and their strong *Cortes*, their tradition of law and representation, and their stress on the binding nature of the contractual relationship between the ruler and the ruled. In Castile, however, the *Cortes* remained weak, unable to thwart the king. The Catalans, by using their own language and by accentuating their unity, cohesiveness, and sense of distinctiveness, had widened the gulf; like the Valencians and the Aragonese, they regarded the Castilians as foreigners, outsiders. In the seventeenth century, when the Catalans talked of Spaniards, they meant Castilians; they referred to themselves as Catalans.[3] In this period of escalating decentralization and federalism, more and more power, both political and economic, gravitated to the provinces.

The crumbling of the power of the central government paralleled the loss of military and imperial hegemony in the seventeenth century. The humiliating defeat at Rocroi, the loss of Portugal, the Franche-Comté, the United Provinces, and Saint Domingue seemed to underscore Spanish impotence. Only a few realized that the loss of these lands could only reduce the financial drain and ultimately benefit the state. By 1700 the small size of the military—the army had only twenty thousand men, the navy only twenty seaworthy vessels—underscored the defenselessness of most of Spain, a Spain ill prepared to defend what was left of the empire.

Economically and demographically, the picture is brighter. On the debit side, a great part of the royal revenues never reached the treasury during Charles II's reign, for these were already pledged to pay off government loans and annuities. Economically, Spain had never been strong even under the able governance of a Philip II. Castile, barely self-sufficient in agriculture, depended heavily on the export of wool. The much maligned Mesta, the sheep-owning guild, played an important role in the economy, for the peasants had both to farm and to herd sheep to survive. Not only government policy but economic exigency dictated the switch to sheep, which were readily marketable and could quickly supply badly needed capital. The decline of the Mesta did not affect agriculture favorably but only damaged the textile industry by leaving it more vulnerable. The need to export wool made Spain in effect a colonial market, for Spain exported raw materials (wool) and imported finished goods (textiles). In Aragon, for example, 78 percent of the exports to France in 1675 consisted of wool and over 51 percent of French imports, textiles.[4] Thus Spain remained dependent on foreign markets in France, Italy, and the Low Countries. The discovery of the New World had worsened the situation, for the bullion imported caused an inflation that made Spanish goods even more expensive and less competitive in foreign markets. Foreign goods, especially from France, dominated and continued to dominate the peninsula.

Under Charles II, however, Spain, especially the periphery of the peninsula, did recover economically. Historians have often equated Castile's decline with that of Spain, but the fiscal and political conditions of the other areas of Spain did not necessarily mirror those of Castile. All signs point to the recovery of the Mediterranean and Cantabrian lands before that of Castile. This was especially true in Catalonia, where the agricultural renaissance and the demographic recovery of the sixteenth century were not interrupted, and where industry thrived as a result of the freedom of trade established in 1659 by the Treaty of the Pyrenees. A comparison between Barcelona and Seville only substantiates this hypothesis. In Barcelona, the volume of trade almost doubled between 1600 and 1700. In Seville trade reached only 10 percent of what it had been in 1600. The guilds still prospered in the late seventeenth century in both Valencia and Catalonia, but in Castile they had undergone a sharp decline. As the industrial recession in Castile led to a reduction in labor demands, the guilds tried to entrench themselves further, becoming agents of obstruction and oppression.

The monetary autonomy of Aragon, Valencia, and Catalonia also helped to account for the differing growth rates. Both Valencia and Catalonia escaped from the inflation of the seventeenth century, which ruined Castile. The shortage of silver led the Castilian authorities to reduce the amount of silver in the vellon and later eliminate it entirely, circulating instead pure copper coins, causing the "copper revolution." This "copper revolution" coupled with the ever-increasing circulation of more and more coins led to spiraling inflation. The government did not remedy this until 1680, when it limited the minting of vellon. In 1686 the government revalued silver, and still later it completely stopped the minting of vellon in order to encourage manufacturing and to instill greater confidence in the government's ability to moderate inflation. Catalonia's industrial, commercial, and agricultural recovery began well before that of Castile—in the 1670s, possibly earlier. The recovery in Valencia dates from the 1690s. But the end of the seventeenth century marked a period of recuperation, lessening inflation, and rising agricultural prices for all of Spain. As a result of good weather and more labor, agricultural output expanded, more land was cultivated, and rent levels, so long depressed, rose.

Demographically Spain also recovered. In Castile the population decline did not persist throughout the seventeenth century but centered on the first half. The long drought years of the late sixteenth and early seventeenth centuries meant an undernourished population, one ill equipped to resist the ravages and eventual spread of the plague. The epidemics that ravaged Castile from 1676 to 1685, killing perhaps a quarter of a million, and the subsistence crisis in 1699 did restrict Castile's growth. Nevertheless, by the end of the seventeenth century the Castilian population had started to stabilize and expand. In contrast, the Cantabrian and Mediterranean provinces were not seriously affected by the epidemics and recovered a full generation earlier.[5]

At the outset, these diverse lands, particularly Castile, welcomed Philip. Philip's popularity there led many to label him a "Castilian king" and strengthened Philip's resolve not to vacate the throne. Uncompromisingly he told his grandfather, Louis XIV, that he would leave Spain only when he was dead and that he preferred to perish "fighting for it foot by foot" at the head of his troops rather than abdicate.[6] As Philip had said, he had "made his choice." No temptation would ever induce him to abandon Spain, which he considered a gift of God.[7] Throughout the war Castile remained unswervingly loyal to him, making it impossible for the allies to retain Castile or even send messengers through the land. Although the allies had twice seized Madrid in 1706 and 1710, they could not hold it because of popular support for Philip. Basically Castile identified the struggle to defend its hegemony in Spain with the Bourbons. It was in Castile that the defenses were built up and the armies supplied. The allied capture of Puerto de Santa Maria with its attendant pillaging and sacrileges, though an isolated incident, only confirmed Castilian prejudices, as did the presence of "heretics" in Charles's army. Although Charles behaved generously toward the Spaniards and though the allies tried to win them over, even to the extent of practicing their Protestant rites in private to avoid stirring up religious hatred, they never succeeded in shaking Castilian loyalty to Philip. It was in Castile that Philip and his popular queen resided; in the other realms Philip remained an absentee ruler. In the words of one Catalan, Philip was a king "chosen by the Castilians." This feeling was understandable in Valencia, where Philip never went at all, and in Aragon, where he spent only a few days, but not so comprehensible in Catalonia, where he spent six months. But then the Catalans, with their experience of French rule in the mid-century and their all too recent suffering at the hands of French troops in the Nine Years' War, had good reason to hate the French. Even though the Catalans in particular resented the French, they initially accepted Philip.

Philip and his advisers, however, rapidly dissipated the goodwill that the people had extended to their new ruler. The shortsighted, tactless, and illegal policies of Philip's ministers exacerbated the fear of Bourbon absolutism and deepened the traditional Francophobia. Long-standing grievances, especially resentment of Castilian dominance, also played a role. In many ways, the civil war manifested what a contemporary, the Marques de San Felipe, described as "the natural aversion of Catalonians, Aragonese, and Valencians to Castile."[8] The pressures brought on by war and very real social inequities fueled the tradition of separatism and caused the insurrection in the eastern half of the peninsula in favor of Charles, the Habsburg claimant to the throne. But the situation was even more complex, for the populace identified with and was loyal to the *comarca* (district), not the larger political groupings. Regional and local rivalries further polarized the country, making the struggle even more bloody and destructive.[9] In Valencia and Aragon some of the *comarcas* and cities such as Morella remained, at great cost, loyal to Philip. Even more significant, the nobility and the common people often had conflicting loyalties. In Castile, the higher nobility proved indifferent, if not hostile, to the Bourbons, while the lower classes actively supported Philip. Don Juan Tomas Enriquez de Cabrera, duque de Medina de Rioseco, admiral of Castile, and Don Luis de la Cerda, duque de Medinaceli, were but two of many who joined Archduke Charles. In Aragon, particularly in Valencia, the situation was reversed: the lower classes supported Charles, the nobility Philip.[10]

In large part, however, necessity rather than conviction accounted for the defection from the Bourbon cause and the loyalty to Charles, for the lands were defenseless against the allies. Charles landed in Catalonia in August 1705 and by the end of that year had taken the cities of Valencia, Barcelona, Saragossa, Cartagena, Ibiza, and Majorca. In the eastern half of Spain few towns could remain loyal to Philip, for they did not have the means to withstand allied forces. For the past two centuries Spain had fought abroad or at the frontiers but not in the heartland, and she was not prepared for the allied onslaught. The bankruptcy of the exchequer and the military ineptitude of the ruling classes necessitated French control of the war effort. Although Philip's government undertook crucial reforms, the war progressed too rapidly. Undoubtedly, the "parlous defences" of the Spanish contributed in no small way to the allies' success, not necessarily the Spanish readiness to welcome

Charles as king as the allies alleged. As late as the 1690s, it was noted that Castile, one of the better-garrisoned parts of Spain, had "insufficient ships and soldiers for our defence [and that] in most towns one can hardly find a musket, arquebus, or pike."[11] In Aragon the viceroy would complain of the "poor and needy state to which the garrisons of this realm had been reduced."[12] In Saragossa the arsenal had no artillery. In Catalonia the situation was little better. Contemporaries described the soldiers as "all starving and deserting as fast as they can."[13] The crucial problem for Philip was not men but supplies. As one soldier put it, "the magazines lacked munitions, the arsenals... were empty."[14] The oft-reiterated criticism that the infantry and cavalry lacked arms, clothing, food, shelter, and pay proved only too true, as the desertion of Spanish troops on the Portuguese frontier attests. As late as April 1705 a French marshal, the comte de Tessé, would compare Spain to a badly harnessed plow "where everything passes without order, without precaution, without decision, without money, without objects." Tessé goes on to say that the duke of Gramont, a French commander, had worn out his lungs and he his patience. He undoubtedly exaggerated when he maintained that he would "not trust a Spaniard, however brave, with the defence of a steeple."[15] But in some cases Philip not only did not send troops but actually withdrew them, as in Valencia, where the populace was left outraged and defenseless. The capitulation of towns like Orihuela owed a great deal to their sense of military insecurity. Yet it must also be acknowledged that the other lands did not want "foreign," that is, Castilian or French, troops because of their frequently criminal behavior. If Philip did not adequately garrison his kingdom, the different lands also made no serious attempt to defend themselves. After the allies took over, they repaired and rebuilt the fortifications, making it more difficult for the Bourbons to retake them later. They not only equipped the garrisons but often left behind allied troops to stiffen local resistance, as at Játiva.[16]

But even considering the defenselessness of Spain, the attitude of the populace, who often rioted in favor of the allies, made defense unthinkable, and Philip's supporters found the enemy without and within. Francophobia had deep roots within Spain. The Francophobia stemmed in part from the constant state of war with France, French economic dominance, and the large and very visible presence of the French, who formed the largest immigrant group in Spain. Even though the character of French immigration changed after 1660 as more specialists and fewer laborers flooded Spain, the greatest insult one could hurl would be the allegation that someone was part French.[17] In the tradition-bound societies of early modern Europe, societies of scarcity and inequity, people feared and hated outsiders. They vented their frustrations on those who did not belong to the community, in this case the French. The Spanish often singled out the French because of the large number in Spain—in Valencia alone in 1691 there were a number of merchants and artisans, estimated at between twelve and twenty-three thousand—and because of the damage inflicted by the French during the wars in the seventeenth century. The Valencian littoral with its relatively large French population and its geographical exposure to the Mediterranean proved particularly susceptible to such violence, especially when the French navy attacked the coast. During the naval bombardment of Alicante in 1691, for example, mobs rioted, murdering Frenchmen, even sacrilegiously slaying those who took refuge in the convent of the Carmelites.[18] In large cities where the French were concentrated, anti-French riots recurred throughout the seventeenth century—in Saragossa in 1694, in Valencia in 1678 and 1691. During wartime, even the government at Madrid declared reprisals against French residents. The outrages perpetrated by French troops intensified the traditional Francophobia. The expulsion, maltreatment, and murder of Frenchmen in Aragon after the allies seized those lands speaks tellingly of the local attitude toward the French.

The Aragonese feared that Bourbon absolutism would endanger their traditional liberties, their *fueros*. The memory of the independence enjoyed in Aragon under the last Habsburg did not endear the Bourbons, with their reforming and absolutist pretensions, to the Aragonese. In 1705, just as earlier in 1640, the transition from an essentially passive to a more active interventionist government, motivated in part by the needs of war, awakened fears of absolutism and the infringement of traditional liberties. Because Philip as king of Castile had no right to billet either French or even Castilian troops without permission, the presence of these troops, even their passage through Aragon, alarmed those who feared for their traditional liberties. When such troops attempted to cross the Aragonese border, trouble predictably ensued. The Aragonese demanded the traditional payments for the passage of troops. When some refused to pay they were denied entry. Still others, though they did pay, were taken by the angry Aragonese over a circuitous route across the kingdom. During the revolt in Aragon, cries of "protect our *fueros* and leave no Frenchman alive" reflected the populace's hatred of France and aversion to Bourbon absolutism. Philip V's ill-conceived and perhaps unknowing violation of certain basic rights such as the quartering of foreign troops, the levying of taxes to support Castilian armies, and the appointment of Castilians to important administrative posts in Aragon alarmed the populace and fueled anti-French sentiment.[19]

The feeling against the French was probably most intense in Catalonia. Ironically, in both origin and language, Catalonia could be said to be more French than Spanish. The conquests of Charlemagne and Louis the Pious had formed the nucleus of Catalonia. At one time the Catalan counts had extended their control over large portions of southern France. The Catalan language was closer to Provençal than Castilian. But the Catalan experience with France during the rebellion of the mid-seventeenth century and the French depredations during the Nine Years' War had disillusioned many. The Catalans found French rule (1640–1652) even worse than Castilian dominance, for the French acted as an occupation force, disregarding their earlier promises to maintain and provision French troops in the principality themselves and continually demanding both money and provisions. The situation only deteriorated when the French viceroy ignored the Catalan constitution and *fueros*.[20] The French retention of Rosseló, Conflent, and thirty-three villages of Cerdanya, approximately one-fifth of the territory and population of traditional Catalonia, at the Peace of the Pyrenees exacerbated relations. Later during the Nine Years' War, the Catalans suffered so greatly at French hands, particularly during the heavy bombardment of Barcelona, that they enthusiastically welcomed the hated Castilian troops. The Catalan nobility in particular resented the French and remained loyal to the Habsburg dynasty. The upper orders had neither forgotten nor forgiven the French for supporting the Catalan peasant uprising of 1688.[21] Louis had thereby succeeded in alienating the very populace whose support his grandson would need so desperately later.

The Catalans associated the French not only with aggression but with absolutism as well. The refrain "privileges or death" reflected the conviction of many Catalans that a decentralized government best preserved the liberties of all of Spain. In their view they were "fighting for ourselves and for all of the Spanish nation."[22] The Catalans remained fiercely loyal to the Habsburgs. Charles II, the last Habsburg, had given titles and honors to non-Castilians, many of them Catalans, counterbalancing the hegemony of Madrid; he had encouraged, not suppressed, Catalan particularism.[23] It was Charles II, also, who had accepted their objections to the viceroy nominated by the crown and who agreed to send instead Prince George of Hesse-Darmstadt. George, the queen's cousin and a winning personality, would play an important role in the fortunes of yet another Habsburg, Charles III.

The Catalans also resented French economic exploitation. During the earlier mid-seventeenth-century revolt, the French attempted to turn the principality into a "French colony" by virtually monopolizing all trade. Many French merchants built up vast fortunes at the expense of local merchants, who had lost their usual outlets in Sicily and Sardinia. In 1705 many Catalans hoped to recover the territory lost to France in 1659 and tried yet again to limit French economic preponderance by setting up their own company, the New Gibraltar Company, to trade with the New World.[24]

Economic resentment was not, however, confined to Catalonia. It was extensive throughout Aragon, whose economy was more closely tied to France than to Castile, but it existed in Castile as well.[25] Although other foreigners, notably the Dutch and the English, also traded extensively with Spain, French predominance made them the obvious target. In the lucrative trade with America, which officially and theoretically was the exclusive monopoly of Spain, the French held 25 percent, the Genoese 21 percent, the Dutch 19 percent, the Flemings 11 percent, the English 11 percent, the Hamburgers 7.6 percent, and the Spaniards 3.8 percent in 1691. A contemporary was not far wrong when as early as 1619 he complained that "nine out of ten parts of the Indies trade are carried out by foreigners."[26] In 1670 one-third of all foreign goods leaving Cadiz for America were French. As one contemporary sarcastically noted, "What better Indies could France have than Spain itself?"[27] The French increasingly skewed the trade balance heavily in their favor. Attempts were made in Aragon, for example, to shake off French dominance by limiting the export of wool, banning the importation of foreign textiles, and expelling the French in the 1670s. But these attempts failed and the trade imbalance persisted throughout the eighteenth century. The French consistently exported more goods to Spain than they imported. Of their exports to Europe, the French directed approximately 75 percent to just two countries, Spain and Italy.

The apogee of French economic power came predictably with the war. Even though the French continued to trade with the Dutch down to 1710, they persuaded the Spanish to prohibit all trade with the allies, especially the English and the Dutch, as early as 1702. In effect France attempted to exclude the rest of Europe from trade with Spain during the war. This effort, however, was doomed to fail because the allies controlled the coast and half the peninsula. The French also tried, unsuccessfully, to suppress and monopolize certain basic industries such as textiles, to participate in the lucrative tobacco and cacao trade, and to establish a joint Franco-Spanish trading company with the Indies. During the earlier part of his reign, Philip accorded the French favored-nation treatment: he allowed many French goods in duty-free, prohibiting the Spanish officials from boarding and searching French ships; he permitted the French to trade freely with Africa but not with the Indies; and he granted them exemption from the extraordinary taxes levied on both foreign residents and natives. The Spanish, however, consistently resisted all French attempts to dominate trade with America, preferring, in the words of a disgruntled Spaniard, to "lose the American trade before consenting to France's deriving the slightest benefit from it."[28] But sheer necessity forced the Spanish colonists to trade with the French, whose piracy only a few years earlier could not easily be forgotten. Although the French did not completely monopolize all trade with Spain or extinguish rival industries, they did consolidate their hold to the extent that after the war Franco-Spanish trade continued to expand.[29]

The traditional Francophobia, fueled by fear of the loss of *fueros* and economic dominance, was exacerbated by Bourbon policy during the war. At the outset the Spanish deplored the excesses of the French troops who had crossed the Spanish border in February 1704. The Bourbon military failures in Spain, particularly the loss of Barcelona, the presence of "parasitic" French ministers in Madrid, and the continuous intrigues at court, discredited Philip. The canny French field marshal, James Fitz-James, duke of Berwick, blamed the ministry at Madrid for not having the ability to foresee the insurrections or the sense to remedy them.[30] Louis XIV's order to the French troops to leave Spain in 1709 at such a desperate time for Philip only lent credence to the widespread belief that France had decided to betray Spain at the subsequent peace. Even Castilians blamed France for the mismanagement of the war.[31]

Yet some Spaniards did admire France and Louis XIV, especially in Madrid, where the presence of and intrigues among the Germans had discredited the Habsburgs, as had the incompetence of the government under Charles II. Witness the duke of Abrantes, announcing the will of Charles II and maliciously embracing and humiliating the Habsburg minister Count Harrach, avowing, "Sir, it is with the greatest pleasure—Sir, it is with the greatest satisfaction—for my whole life I take my leave of the most illustrious House of Austria."[32] For many, France offered the only hope of preserving the Spanish Empire. Realizing the necessity of drastic measures, they endorsed Bourbon reform plans. Although they adopted French customs and fashions, they often despised the French coteries at Madrid and distrusted Louis's commercial and diplomatic schemes. Most of the aristocracy, the higher clergy, and the important state officials remained loyal to Philip even in Aragon. Yet the Bourbon regime rapidly disillusioned an important segment of the nobility. By excluding the nobles from playing an effective role in either the government or the army, Philip had thwarted the ambitions of many. Loyalty to the Habsburg dynasty, Bourbon military disasters, personal resentment, loss of needed income, disenchantment with some of Philip's ministers such as Portocarrero, family loyalty, and resentment of the "insatiable ambition of the French dynasty"[33] convinced many to join Charles. Four of the twelve grandees of the first class defected to the Habsburgs. Philip had not wanted to undermine the aristocracy, merely to break the power of the grandees, to eliminate an irresponsible group from power and replace it instead with centralized responsibility, using ministers who worked through the secretaries of state. In most cases the nobles did not suffer greatly for their disloyalty. The Treaty of Vienna (April 1725) signed between Austria and Spain provided for the restoration of their property, eliminating some of the lingering resentments left by the war. Generally the reforms initiated by the Bourbons did not greatly affect the nobility, who still retained their seigneurial rights.[34]

The war even divided the clergy. The vast majority in Castile supported Philip, using the pulpit to promote the Bourbon cause, celebrating Philip's victories, such as Villaviciosa, as judgments of God, explicitly comparing such battles to earlier victories against the infidel, such as Lepanto. Some of the more extreme went so far as to label Habsburg partisans perjurers and heretics. In general throughout Aragon the Jesuits supported Philip; the Mendicants, Charles. At the end of the war many of the Habsburg supporters went into exile in either Vienna or Italy.[35]

In Valencia Charles derived most of his support from the lower clergy and peasants—an often explosive combination that would recur again and again throughout Spanish history. The illusory hope of reducing their seigneurial obligations combined with their hatred of the French convinced many to align with Charles.[36] The peasants had grievances not only against the local nobility but against the king as well. But in the eastern provinces the king had little influence and that often only indirect through the appointment of viceroys and important officials. The places where the king had direct jurisdiction were extremely limited. In Valencia, for example, out of the 560 towns, only 33 belonged to the king. His power was limited, then, in Valencia, where the insurrection assumed more the character of a social struggle than anywhere else, where the peasants were particularly oppressed. There the lord took as much as one-third of the serfs' produce. The rebellion in Valencia had its roots in the reign of Philip IV, who resettled Christian peasants on the land after the expulsion of the Moriscos. The king eliminated the system of free landholding and replaced it with a seigneurial regime where the lords controlled the land and taxes. Those lords subjected the peasantry to the most onerous terms and granted them only usufruct of the land. In 1693 the peasants refused to pay taxes, turned to banditry, and revolted. By comparison, the lot of the Catalan peasant was not as oppressive, but it was miserable enough. Those conditions impelled them to look to the crown for redress and often to revolt. After swarms of locusts destroyed the harvest of 1687, the villages in Catalonia in 1688–1689 refused to billet troops or to pay the *donativo*, a tax. They staged the biggest rural uprising in seventeenth-century Spain, the "revolt of the barretines." The crown never succeeded in completely extinguishing these revolts. The widespread and illegal possession of firearms, the collusion with bandits, and the attacks on tax officials merely reflected the pervasiveness of violence throughout the countryside.

The nobility did not limit their exactions to the countryside but also extended them to the boroughs, which they also controlled. Taxation fell heaviest on the small holder because so many others were exempt from taxation. The taxpayer owed the tithe, approximately 10 percent, to the church; land rents, often the biggest burden, and one that had progressively risen in the seventeenth century as the arable land had been extended; seigneurial taxes—difficult to calculate, but usually higher, sometimes as much as three times higher than that paid to the state; government taxes; and debt, either individual or municipal. Though both the cost of living and the price of grain had risen 300 percent during the seventeenth century, taxes had risen even higher, 400 percent. The government's periodic attempts to reduce taxes had little effect on an overburdened, indebted peasantry. It was this indebtedness which bound both peasants and townmen in an ever-spiraling cycle of poverty and impelled them to rebel. In the cities, when the demands of the populace for changes in the civic administration, as at Ubeda and Calahorra; direct political concessions, as in Catalonia; or abrogation of seigneurial levies were not met, revolt broke out.

The allies took advantage of the existing social discontent. The fracture lines of the society, already strained, widened, and in some cases, such as Valencia, split apart. In Catalonia, the differences within the bourgeoisie intensified and contributed to the unrest. In Barcelona the commercial bourgeoisie sought to defend their privileges against the petty bourgeoisie and against interlopers, that is, those named directly by the crown. Their collective demand for certain privileges from Philip V, such as honorary citizenship, reflected their aspirations for noble status. Such stances mirrored the collective rivalries present before and exacerbated by the war.[37] In the kingdom of Valencia, for example, the allies, aided by the parish priests, garnered peasant support for Charles. Astutely, the allies used outlaws, men who had been literally outside the law, to appeal to the peasants, who often resented the authorities. Throughout the early modern period, the lower classes often mythologized outlaws who, according to popular legend at least, righted wrongs and helped the powerless.[38] The allies put ashore Francisco García de Avila, one of the leaders of the peasant revolt of 1693, and Juan Bautista y Ramos, a former carpenter, to enlist the support of the rural masses. These two promised the peasants freedom from taxation and from onerous servile obligations. The allies had no trouble, for example, taking Játiva, the center of the earlier peasant insurrection in 1693 and the site of a virtually indefensible, undermanned, and undergunned garrison. The ruling classes there had supported Philip, while the lower allied with Charles. Popular disaffection undoubtedly played a large role in the fall of other cities such as Valencia. The subsistence crises in 1706 and again in 1710 triggered by the poor harvest of 1705 and the disastrous rains of 1709 fed that discontent. Hunger moved the masses. Throughout Aragon the populace rioted and often forced the Bourbon troops to withdraw. In Saragossa on the Feast of the Holy Innocents (25 December 1705), Frenchmen passing through the city were beaten and murdered, prompting Spaniards to remark that the kingdom was being "watered by the blood of the king's troops."[39] Throughout the eastern half of the peninsula this pattern was repeated again and again; the upper and middle classes supported the Bourbons, the lower the Habsburgs.

One of the few exceptions to this was in Catalonia. Unlike 1640 the peasants' resistance was not decisive, and many Catalan villages included Philip's adherents.[40] The Catalan merchants, who vied with the French, hoped to establish a "new Cadiz," to transform Catalonia into another Holland. Charles also won over the "petite noblesse," who resented the "Castilianization" of the greater nobility, and the members of the *Cortes* and the municipalities, who wanted to protect their *fueros*. Both the middle classes and the lower nobility fought to defend their political liberties and to promote their economic interests.

Charles also exploited the well-known separatism in Aragon, especially in Catalonia. In this Philip played into his hands. Philip had proved coldly indifferent to the *fueros* of Valencia and had not even attempted to hold a *Cortes* there as he had in Aragon and Catalonia. He gave the Valencians no opportunity to present their grievances or to see their new sovereign. He had also flagrantly violated the rights of the Aragonese by sending troops into that land without obtaining permission first. Philip's ministers were blindly unaware of the difficulties inherent in getting money from Aragon, which had no legal obligation to pay taxes to support Castilian troops. The tactless request for a *donativo voluntario* in 1705 is but one instance of the shortcomings of his policy. He blundered on by appointing a Castilian, the conde de San Esteban de Gormas, to the viceroyalty of Aragon, a post that his predecessor, Charles II, had promised to the Aragonese. By contrast, in Catalonia the Habsburgs had earlier adopted a policy of conciliation and appointed Don Juan José of Austria, Philip IV's son, as viceroy of the province in 1677. Both Don Juan and the nobles on the Council of Aragon, the executive body for the three realms of Aragon, made concessions to the Aragonese, prompting one Catalan historian to conclude that Charles II was the best king Spain ever had.[41] Where the Habsburgs had earlier conciliated, Philip alienated. In Catalonia, Philip illegally dismissed the current viceroy and appointed Portocarrero's nephew before even taking his oath as king. The popular support for the conde de Cifuentes indicated how much Philip had already alienated Aragon and how deeply they feared for their liberties. The local bishop was unable to arrest the conde, a prominent noble who had joined the Habsburg cause, because the people identified him with the preservation of their *fueros*. The position of and support for Cifuentes echoed that of another prominent noble in an earlier affair under Philip II in the 1590s. Antonio Perez, a secretary of Philip II, had fled to Aragon after his arrest and claimed the right to be tried by a local court. Both Perez and Cifuentes embodied, in the eyes of the people, a defense of local liberty. Philip V fulfilled their worst suspicions. Philip's decision to revoke the *fueros* of Aragon in 1707 and his ministers' readiness to treat all Aragonese as rebels, even though many had not sided with Charles, angered many.

Archduke Charles, on the other hand, had done all he could to win over the populace; he expelled French traders, reduced taxation, abolished feudal dues, and generously rewarded his followers with pensions and appointments, thus making the subsequent reconquest even more difficult for Philip. Throughout the war, prices did not rise significantly, except in Catalonia, where there was great inflation. In Barcelona and Valencia the presence of the allies caused a temporary boom. The war also did not greatly affect population growth. Catalonia, the most devastated area, went through a period of stagnation, but not significant decline, in part because the allies took such care to win over the populace and because this war was not—as was true of so many others—marked by epidemics and plagues.

Politically, the war proved more devastating. After the Bourbon victory at Almanza (1707), only Catalonia remained in Charles's hand. The way lay open for the Bourbon conquest of most of Aragon and Valencia. From the first, the government adopted a policy of reprisal; Philip eliminated the *fueros*; he forced the populace to pay Castilian taxes, to billet a foreign army, to obey foreign laws and foreign officials, and to use a foreign currency—Castilian. The government disarmed the whole population and sacked recalcitrant cities like Játiva. Berwick ultimately razed that city to the ground in order to, in his words, "impress with terror and to prevent by such a severe example similar obstinacy."[42] He exiled the remaining inhabitants to Castile and left only one building standing, a church. The Bourbon policy proved particularly harsh in Valencia, the first area to be reconquered.[43] The government levied, but later was forced to repeal, excessively high taxes there. In Aragon, Philip established a royal monopoly in both salt and tobacco. In Catalonia, monarchical absolutism also triumphed; the king reshaped the municipal organizations and placed all political and judicial power in the *audiencia* (tribunal), eventually reorganizing Catalonia under the Nova Planta of 1716. As a precautionary measure, the government ordered the disarming of the civil population and the expulsion of many of Charles's supporters, most notably the ecclesiastics. In spite of these preventive actions, rebellion flickered briefly again in the interior in 1719.[44]

The Catalans, relying on the false promises of the allies, had been the last to be reconquered. In 1705, just as in 1640, fierce resentment of Castilian dominance in Spain had persuaded many to revolt. In both instances, the Catalans sought to defend and preserve the *fueros*. In 1705, however, the Catalans fought not for separatism but for greater freedom for all of Spain.[45] In 1705 the movement was "offensive" in the sense that the Catalans hoped to reconquer the rest of the peninsula for the Habsburgs, while in 1640 the separatists had been in a primarily defensive position. Even after Charles had agreed to withdraw all imperial troops from Catalonia (March 1713) and his wife had left (July 1713), the Catalans still refused unconditional submission and continued fighting on—but hopelessly. The Spanish, reinforced by the French, began a general assault on Barcelona on 11 September. Even when the Franco-Spanish troops had breached the walls and the inhabitants realized that no outside aid would be forthcoming, they fought on with desperation, amazing the soldiers with their tenacity. Only after more than 9,700 citizens had been killed did the Bourbons succeed in conquering this last stronghold.[46] The allies not only had refused to aid the Catalans but had been ready to use their troops to force the city to surrender. The capture of Barcelona saved the allies from this ignominy, and the revolt against Philip ended with bloody reprisals.

NOTES

1. Antonio Domínguez Ortiz, *Sociedad y estado en el siglo xvii español* (Barcelona, 1976), p. 24.

2. Philip Wayne Powell, *The Tree of Hate: Propaganda and Prejudices Affecting United States Relations with the Hispanic World* (London, 1961), p. 6.

3. B.M., Add. Mss. 28, 915, fols. 99–101, Ellis to Stanhope, 21 December 1703; Add. Mss. 37, 351, fols. 217–218, Hedges to Whitworth, 21 December 1703 and in P.R.O., S.P. Germany, 105/71/51; B.M., Add. Mss. 31, 132, fol. 37, Raby's Letter of 26 January 1704, Berlin and fol. 39, Raby to Hill, Berlin, 26 January 1704; Alg. Rijks., Arch. Staten Generaal 6587, Hamel-Bruynincx Report of 19 February 1704.

4. Henry Kamen, "The Decline of Spain: A Historical Myth," *Past and Present* 81 (November 1978): 45; Henry Kamen, *Spain in the Later Seventeenth Century* (New York, 1980), pp. 67–112; Jaime Vicens Vives, *An Economic History of Spain* (Princeton, N.J., 1969), pp. 411–467.

5. Pierre Vilar, *La Catalogne dans l'Espagne moderne: Recherches sur les fondements économiques des structurales nationales* (Paris, 1962), 1:588–670; Kamen, *Spain... Seventeenth Century*, pp. 39–66.

6. Henry Kamen, *Spain, 1469–1714: A Society of Conflict* (New York, 1983), pp. 264–265.

7. William Coxe, *Memoires of The Kings of Spain... 1700–1788* (London, 1815), 2:107.

8. Domínguez Ortiz, *Sociedad y estado*, p. 37.

9. Ibid., pp. 39–40; Kamen, *The War of the Succession*, pp. 17, 22, 248–249; Kamen, *Spain... Seventeenth Century*, p. 6.

10. Domínguez Ortiz, *Sociedad y estado*, pp. 40–42.

11. Kamen, *The War of the Succession*, p. 57.

12. Ibid., p. 57.

13. Wolfgang Michael, "The Treaties of Partition and the Spanish Succession," *The Cambridge Modern History*, 5:375.

14. Kamen, *The War of the Succession*, p. 58.

15. Coxe, *Spain*, 1:340; also refer to 341, 343.

16. Kamen, *The War of the Succession*, pp. 57–60, 263, 290–298.

17. J. Nadal and E. Giralt, *La Population catalane de 1553 à 1717: L'Immigration française et les autres facteurs de son développement* (Paris, 1960), pp. xiv, 85–87.

18. Sabastià Garcia Martinez, *Els fonaments del pais Valencia modern* (Valencia, 1968), pp. 103–125.

19. Ibid., pp. 11, 45, 52, 54, 91, 125–128, 252–258; Kamen, *Spain... Seventeenth Century*, pp. 182–189; Vives, *Spain*, pp. 419–422, 432–435.

20. José Sanabre, *La acción de Francia en Cataluña en la pugna por la hegemonía de Europe 1640–1659* (Barcelona, 1976).

21. Henry Kamen, "A Forgotten Insurrection of the Seventeenth Century: The Catalan Peasant Rising of 1688," *Journal of Modern History* 49 (June 1977):230.

22. Vilar, *La Catalogne*, 1:679.

23. Ibid., 1:670–672.

24. Roger B. Merriman, *Six Contemporaneous Revolutions* (London, 1963), pp. 1–10; J. H. Elliott, *The Revolt of the Catalans: A Study in the Decline of Spain (1598–1640)* (London, 1963), pp. 535–537; J. H. Elliott, "Revolts in the Spanish Monarchy," in *Preconditions of Revolution in Early Modern Europe*, edited by Robert Forster and Jack P. Greene (Baltimore, 1970), pp. 109–130; Vilar, *La Catalogne*, 1:625–638.

25. Kamen, "The Decline of Spain," p. 45.
26. Vives, *Spain*, pp. 433; also refer to Geoffrey J. Walker, *Spanish Politics and Imperial Trade, 1700–1789* (Bloomington, Ind., 1979), pp. 140–196.
27. Kamen, "The Decline of Spain," p. 44.
28. Parker, *Spanish Politics and Imperial Trade*, p. 23; also refer to pp. 1–63 and to George Scelle, *La Traité negrière aux indes de Castille* (Paris, 1906), 2:141–451, for French economic policy during the war and for the Spanish hostility to commercial union with France.
29. Vives, *Spain*, pp. 432–438; Kamen, *War of the Succession*, pp. 140–196.
30. James Fitz-James, duke of Berwick, *Mémoires du maréchal de Berwick* (Switzerland, 1778), 1:183.
31. Ibid., pp. 11, 45, 52, 54, 91, 125–128, 252–258; Kamen, *Spain . . . Seventeenth Century*, pp. 182–189; Vives, *Spain*, pp. 419–422, 432–435.
32. Kamen, *War of the Succession*, p. 5.
33. Pedro Voltes Bou, *La Guerra de sucesíon en Valencia* (Valencia, 1964), p. 30.
34. Ibid., pp. 94–107.
35. Domínguez Ortiz, *Sociedad y estado*, p. 20.
36. See, for example, Voltes Bou, *Valencia*, pp. 15–68, and Domínguez Ortiz, *Sociedad y estado*, pp. 44–45.
37. Pedro Molas Ribalta, *Comerc i estructura social a Catalunya i Valencia als segles xvii i xviii* (Barcelona, 1977), esp. pp. 172–201.
38. Peter Burke, *Popular Culture in Early Modern Europe* (New York, 1978) pp. 165–166.
39. Vilar, *La Catalogne* 1:257; also refer to 195–225, 269–308, 371–375; Hussey and Bromley, "The Spanish Empire."
40. Vilar, *La Catalogne*, 1:673–678.
41. Kamen, "The Catalan Peasant Rising," p. 211.
42. Berwick, *Mémoires*, 1:257.
43. Voltes Bou, *Valencia*, pp. 69–105; for Catalonia refer to Vilar, *La Catalogne*, 1:673–710.
44. Joan Mercader i Riba, *Felipe V i Catalunya* (Barcelona, 1968).
45. Domínguez Ortiz, *Sociedad y estado*, pp. 46–48.
46. Berwick, *Mémoires*, 2:109–125.

5

Conclusions

The insurrections ended as they had begun—with violence: in Hungary the countryside was ravaged by imperial troops; in Spain the Franco-Spanish troops mercilessly assaulted Barcelona, slaughtering over twelve thousand; and in France the rebels were hunted down and ritualistically executed. Violence elicited counterviolence; terror, counterterror. In early modern Europe authorities customarily reacted with repression, the violence of which dehumanized and traumatized the populace. On the other hand, violence gave to the rebel, however temporarily and however illusorily, a sense of control; it freed him from a sense of inaction and despair. This was not surprising in a society accustomed to a high level of violence.

First, all three societies had traditions of protest against the centralized state; in all cases their pasts conditioned their prospects for future violence.[1] Their indestructible past, their historical traditions and beliefs, increased the likelihood and subsequent magnitude of violence. The "permanent and universal preconditon" for violence, "for revolt in every society in early modern Europe [was] the pressure of population on food resources and the ever-present threat of harvest failure and starvation."[2] The levying of new taxes or the raising of old ones could ignite revolt, as could a rise in the price of that basic commodity, bread. Roland Mousnier has argued that it was "above all royal taxation, its weight, the way it was introduced, assessed and collected that gave rise to the revolts" of the seventeenth century.³ The state's attack on local liberties and privileges could also ignite revolt.

During the French religious wars Languedoc, a privileged province and a *pays d'état*, had resisted centralization. Languedoc, an outlying province, had retained a distinctly Mediterranean language and culture long after its integration into the French state. That province, as Charles Tilly has pointed out, played a role in the "popular revolts and great rebellions [that] occurred with remarkable frequency" before the middle of the seventeenth century.⁴ In the 1620s and the 1630s these mountainous areas had often sheltered opposition forces. For example, in 1622 the defeated troops of the duke of Rohan had retreated to the Cévennes. In 1632 the peasants had joined with their lords in defending the province against the central government, whose most visible agent was the tax collector. Languedoc witnessed in the one year of 1644 a fiscal rebellion in Figeac and disorders in Montpellier and Nîmes. Languedoc also participated actively in the post-Fronde rebellions, which centered not in the cities but in the mountains. In the late seventeenth century revolts still erupted, but the private armies and noble leaders no longer played a major role. That role was assumed by citizen militias and commoners. This was certainly true in the Cévennes. The issues had also changed. It was not the traditional economic disputes over taxation, or even the seizure of grain,⁵ that ignited the Camisard revolt but rather religious issues. Even earlier the Waldensians and the Albigensians had fought Catholic orthodoxy. The Protestants in Languedoc had a tradition of protest against the state; witness the rebellions during the reigns of Louis XIII and Louis XIV. For example, from 1621 to 1629 Protestants fought the royal forces. In 1643 armed Protestants gathered at Ribaute, and in 1645 others assembled illegally in Aubenas and still others attacked bishops in Carcassonne and Mende. There were disturbances in the Vivarais in 1653 and in Carcassonne in 1656. The Huguenots of Languedoc continued the century-old struggle against the king even without their great protectors. These local battles did not escalate into rebellion until the government intensified its efforts to stamp out Protestantism. Jean

CONCLUSIONS

Cavalier certainly conceived of the revolt in terms of the past. In his *Mémoires*, he contends that the insurgents throught of themselves as the descendants of the Albigensians and the Vaudois, destined to continue their struggle against superstition and persecution.[6] Interestingly enough, their enemies sometimes dubbed them *barbets*, an allusion to the Vaudois.[7] The Camisards even used the military routes their Protestant predecessors had.[8] But protest during Louis XIV's reign was not confined to Languedoc. Revolts erupted in Boulonnais in 1662, in Chalosse from 1664 to 1670, in the Lower Vivarais in 1670, in Bordeaux and Brittany in 1675 (the so-called stamped paper revolt), in Quercy in 1707, and so on.

Undoubtedly a tradition of protest also existed in Hungary. The Bocskai insurrection of 1605–1606, Gabor Bethlen's wars of 1619–1621 and 1623–1636, György I Rákóczi's war in 1644–1645, the Wesselényi conspiracy of 1671, and the *kuruc* war of 1672–1685 attest to the Hungarian resistance to absolutism. Their grievances were all too real. Throughout the sixteenth and seventeenth centuries three evils, as Nicholas Zrínyi pointed out to Leopold I, plagued Hungary: Turkish raids, religious persecutions, and German mercenaries.[9] By 1703 the Turks no longer greatly endangered the Hungarians or for that matter the Habsburgs, but the other two "evils" remained and helped to ignite the Rákóczi insurrection. Before both the *kuruc* war of the 1670s and the 1680s and the Rákóczi War of Independence, sedition was widespread, reflecting the populace's disaffection with the Habsburg government. The ravages of the imperial troops and the abrogation of the Hungarian constitution incensed many, who argued that the Habsburgs treated Hungary not as a liberated land but as a conquered foe. Such formidable men as Ferenc Wesselényi, Péter Zrínyi, Ferenc Nadasdy, Ferenc Frangipan, and Ferenc I Rákóczi conspired to overthrow the Habsburgs in the 1660s. Apprised beforehand, the Habsburgs easily quashed the so-called *Wesselényi fronde*. Disregarding past practice and Hungarian law, they executed many of its leaders and confiscated the land of others. In 1671 Leopold I went even further, abolishing the office of palatine; establishing a *gubernium*, a committee consisting of the Grand Master of the Teutonic Order, Johann Ampringen, four German and four Hungarian appointees, to rule Hungary; and levying additional taxes.

These reforms coupled with the growth of the Counter-Reformation sparked the Thököli uprising whereas a peasant insurrection ignited the conflict in 1703. Unlike Rákóczi, Thököli was dependent on both French and Ottoman support, whereas Rákóczi garnered only French support. In addition to French subsidies yet another filament that tied both wars together were the numerous Thököli veterans such as Albert Kis, who later served under Rákóczi. Hungary, a frontier land, a border area between the Habsburgs on the west and the Ottomans on the east, witnessed almost continual warfare from 1526, the defeat at Mohács, to 1711, the peace of Szatmár. Thus a large group, a warrior estate, a hereditary stratum of soldiers, existed and persisted generation after generation providing the levies for the popular wars. An exaggerated combativeness and a heroic ethos characterized this military estate in the early modern period. The predominance of military elements and a military mentality led one observer to describe Hungarian history as a "continuous heroic epic."[10]

Violence was pervasive not only in France and Hungary but in Spain as well. These conflicts, generated by economic pressure or the insistence on retaining local liberties, often erupted into revolt. These revolts reveal a great deal about the economic fissures of the society and the pervasive problem of regionalism. In Spain as in the rest of Europe, hunger moved the masses in both town and countryside. A subsistence crisis ignited the troubles in Granada (1648), Cordoba (1652), and Seville (1652). In Vizcaya, for example, revolt broke out in 1631–1632 when the government attempted to levy a salt tax on a populace already decimated by the great famine of 1630. The tax protest soon merged with the issues of economic inequities and "Castilian" rule. After the Basques executed six rebel leaders, withdrew the salt tax, and upheld the local *fueros*, the revolt collapsed. Whether in town or countryside bread shortages and high or inequitable taxes incited men to revolt.[11] But these and other disturbances were but minor tremors in this volcanic society.

The great shocks that endangered the very fabric of Spain took place in the kingdom of Aragon. The revolt in Aragon in 1591, the Catalan revolt in 1640, the revolt of the *segadors* in Catalonia in 1688, and the peasant rebellion in Valencia in 1693 foreshadowed problems that would recur later when the stresses of war during the conflict for the Spanish Succession precipitated a reenactment of earlier crises. Ever since the marriage of Ferdinand and Isabella had dynastically united Castile and Aragon in 1469, the Aragonese had been intent on preserving their privileges, their *fueros*. They greatly resented and resisted the Castilianization of Spain. They took every possible opportunity to resist what they thought of as Castilian incursions. Not surprising then is the warning Charles I gave to his son Philip II that the kingdom of Aragon was much more difficult to rule than the other lands because of the very nature of its privileges and constitutions.[12] Philip discovered just how percipient this advice was when the Aragonese revolted in 1591–1592, precipitating what has been termed the greatest constitutional crisis of his reign. The troubles began when the king, as had his predecessors, appointed a tactless, inept Castilian viceroy for Aragon. The Aragonese protested and argued, quite incorrectly, that their *fueros* stipulated that all royal officials must be Aragonese. The situation deteriorated even further when the king's disgraced minister, Antonio Perez, escaped prison and fled to Saragossa, where he spread the rumor that the king intended to further subvert the *fueros*. Riots ensued in Saragossa but did not spread to the rest of the kingdom. While Perez attempted to garner French support for an uprising, Philip acted, quickly sending troops into the kingdom and publicly executing the leaders who had not escaped to France. Fortunately for Philip and for Aragon, virtually all the cities except Saragossa and Teruel had refused to assist the rebels. Philip did not adopt a punitive policy but did attempt to eliminate the endemic lawlessness, to restore order, and to extend the authority of the king. He did insist upon his right to appoint "foreign" viceroys and to remove the *Justiciar*, whose court's verdicts could not be overruled even by the king.

Philip II had succeeded in strengthening his control over Aragon, but when Philip IV attempted to do the same in Catalonia, the people again revolted, and on a much larger scale. In 1640, when Spain found itself at war with France, Olivares, the Spanish minister, desperately short of funds and troops, tried to pressure the Catalans into contributing both men and money to defend Spain. In his view the devil should "take the constitutions and whoever observes them . . . for no man can observe them who has not been abandoned by God and who is not an enemy of His Divine Majesty, of his king, and of his fatherland."[13] That view was not universally shared. When resistance predictably ensued, Olivares raged that "the Catalans ought to see more of the world than just Catalonia"[14] and attempted to billet troops illegally throughout Catalonia, only to have rioting break out. Order collapsed as bandits, the underprivileged, the landless, the poor rebelled. This "social revolt" soon merged with the political resistance to the abrogation of the *fueros*. The Catalan revolt combined both elite and popular movements; the upper orders joined with the lower and protested the unauthorized taxation. They were united not only in their opposition to Castilian pretensions and policies but also in their desire to avoid the economic disasters that plagued Castile. The basic difference in language between Castile and Catalonia only served to increase the sense of alienation in a land where the tradition of liberty and independence cemented the social framework. Philip also had committed the fatal mistake of antagonizing the ruling class, whose support was essential if the revolt were to succeed. Royal absenteeism undoubtedly also played a part, for the king resided not in Aragon but in Castile. As J. H. Elliott has stressed, the "absence of a father figure in an essentially patriarchal society" helped to "disorient" the society.[15] Disillusioned by and yet at the same time hoping to exploit Spanish weakness as evidenced by Spanish defeats in the Thirty Years' War, the Catalans thought that they had a reasonable chance of winning. Intent on preserving their liberties, on defending their historic identity, the Catalans proclaimed their allegiance to Louis XIII. Mystified, Olivares castigated the Catalans for "having thrown themselves into as complete a rebellion as Holland, without reason or occasion."[16] Yet another contemporary remarked that "only the preachers are missing to make them lose their faith along with their obedience."[17]

Thus Spain found itself not only waging war with France but fighting a civil war as well. Catalonia became a French theater of war. Predictably, French troops, merchants, and goods poured into Catalonia. Taxes increased, the economy stagnated, and food shortages escalated. The populace faced not only economic disaster but famine, malnutrition, and ultimately the plague. It also confronted a French government that proved more arbitrary and exacting than Philip's. The surrender of Barcelona in 1652 effectively ended the revolt. Once Philip had promised to respect the *fueros* and to proclaim a general amnesty, the Catalans, disillusioned with France, returned to their allegiance to Philip. But resentment against France lingered and intensified, particularly after the Treaty of the Pyrenees in 1659 ceded lands east of the Pyrenees to Louis XIV. The repeated incursions of the Sun King's armies in the seventeenth century only deepened this resentment, as did French support of the subsequent uprising of 1688.

The revolt of the barretines (the *barretina* was the cap worn by the Catalan peasants) of 1688–1689, although the largest popular uprising in seventeenth-century Spain, ultimately collapsed because it failed to secure the support of the upper classes. In 1688 the situation in Catalonia was desperate, for locusts had swarmed into the area for the last four years, destroying the crops. The bitterly cold winter of 1688, while destroying the locusts, only added to the privations of the populace. Yet in this difficult situation the government, again confronted with war, attempted to billet troops. Many villages refused, and three members of the *Diputacio* went so far as to protest the billeting of troops and the hardships that would ensue. The viceroy overreacted and ill-advisedly arrested the three and replaced them with new appointees. The situation further deteriorated when the viceroy ordered a detachment of troops to be billeted in Centellas. The resulting rioting, which forced the army to withdraw, reflected the widespread resentment and opposition to billeting, an onerous obligation in the best of times. As one contemporary aptly described the unrest, "the blaze in Centellas has been put out, but the ashes are scattered throughout Catalonia."[18] Both the Catalans and the government avoided further provocative measures. The government, fully cognizant of the desperate condition of the peasantry, adopted the position that "sweet medicine" (conciliation) could only cure, but "sharp medicine" (reprisals) only aggravate the situation in Catalonia. For their part, the Catalan towns agreed to billet the troops but refused to pay the contribution. Meanwhile rural laborers gathered together and marched to Barcelona to demand a reduction of the contribution, release of the imprisoned *Diputacio* members, and a general pardon. As rioting spread throughout Catalonia in June and July, the Council of Aragon reported that the province was "completely out of control."[19] Contemporaries reported that the beleaguered peasantry resented the unfair distribution of the billeted soldiers and the additional burden of paying the contribution. Luckily the harvest was bountiful in 1688 and the conflagration died down in the fall and winter. Meanwhile, as war with France loomed nearer, the Catalan estates agreed to levy the *donativo*, a tax payable only by the lower orders. This decision divided the Catalans, for the higher orders now sided with the government. As in 1640 the French attempted to exploit the situation by using the peasant leaders as French agents to stir up more unrest. Groups of peasants refused to pay the tax and went about disarming, not killing, the soldiers. The new viceroy took a tough, uncompromising stand and sent out troops to quell the insurgents. After one of the leaders, Antoni Soler, a man of wealth and stature in the community was treacherously murdered by his own grandson for the reward, the revolt collapsed. Many of the rebels escaped, some to France, while the others attempted to stir up further unrest.[20]

The second and largest peasant uprising of the entire Habsburg period broke out in Valencia in 1693. This peasant revolt, like many others, was born of desperation. Natural disasters such as locusts, bubonic plague, and earthquakes had aggravated the already deteriorating position of the peasants, who found themselves unable to pay the heavy taxes and to meet the financial exactions of their lords. Heavily indebted, the peasants could not pay the extortionate dues levied in both money and kind. Bound in an onerous, repressive vassalage, many fled, often turning to banditry in order to survive. But, more important, the peasants' convictions that the exactions were illegal were reinforced partly because of the support of lawyers, clergy, and officials, who opposed the exploitative system of vassalage established on the lands after the expulsion of the Moriscos. When the peasantry refused to pay their dues, the government dispatched royal troops to quash them. One of the two main leaders, Francisco García, subsequently escaped, only to return during the War of the Spanish Succession and reignite the revolt.

These insurrections but prefigured the revolts that would erupt during the War of the Spanish Succession. They also reflected the high level of violence pervasive in early modern Spain, as did the illegal but widespread ownership of firearms, the assault on tax collectors, and the collusion with bandits.[21] In both Spain and Hungary the peasants regarded bandits not as outlaws but rather as heroes or avengers, accepting them within the society. As Eric Hobsbawm has stressed, these "social bandits" existed in an agricultural society based on exploitation of the peasantry. In times of profound economic crisis or natural catastrophe, as in Spain and Hungary, banditry became endemic. Such banditry was symptomatic of the crises in early modern society; it was "the precursor or companion of major social movements."[22] In both Hungary and Spain the bandits sought to restore the traditional order; they protested, for example, as Tamas Esze did in Hungary, against unfair taxes such as the salt tax and the portion. Such protest could also be directed against the agents of the lords or the government who attempted to collect these payments, the tax collectors.

The tradition of violent protest was reinforced by the identification of concrete targets, which helped to mobilize support for the insurgents and increased the normative justification for violence. Such targets were vulnerable to attack, for they provided a tangible enemy, unlike the distant and divinely sanctioned king. The peasants could be stirred to act against the tax collector, an alien element in the rural world and the most visible agent of the central government, just as the Protestants could be stirred to act against the local priest. The increasingly bitter and sustained resistance meant that taxes could be collected only by force or by threat of force. Political violence could be normatively justified when the legitimacy of the regime itself was questioned, as was the case in Hungary and Spain.[23] In these two lands the insurrectionists established an alternate authority. Both the Hungarians and the Catalans resented the imposition of what they considered to be foreign institutions. They identified with the kingdom of Aragon and with the kingdom of Hungary, not with the Habsburg empire or Spain. They looked to the smaller unit for their economic being, their cultural identity, and their political liberties. The conditions in Hungary in particular—a borderland between two rival empires, the Habsburgs and the Turks—helped to foster what might be termed a sense of protonationalism. One of Ferenc Rákóczi's lieutenants, Miklós Bercsényi, argued in 1704 that they had taken up arms to "throw off the yoke cruelly imposed by a foreign nation," that they must, with God's help, reestablish "the old glorious liberty of our beloved Fatherland."[24] Undoubtedly the fear or suspicion that the Germans endangered the political rights and economic well-being of the Hungarians worsened the situation. The challenge to power and privilege conditioned the image of the threatening power. Very pragmatic decisions such as Leopold's favoritism toward the Germans only fueled existing resentment. Concrete symbols, such as the *camiso* in France, reinforced the sense of community, the we-versus-them mentality. Slogans such as "liberty of conscience or death," "God, fatherland, and liberty," "protect our *fueros*," and "leave no Frenchman alive" mobilized the masses by articulating grievances and goals. The government's repression could only increase popular support for the rebels. The new ideational justifications for violence were so effective because they were based on a historical tradition of resistance. Furthermore, they appealed to the people in terms of specific deprivations such as the loss of traditional liberties. The liberties they sought were not "powers of themselves but merely an exemption from the abuses of power."[25] What they sought were safeguards against the encroaching power of government. In France they fought for freedom of conscience, in Hungary for protection of age-old rights such as the right to elect the king, and in Spain for the retention of the *fueros* such as those that forbade the quartering of foreign troops.

These three revolts were linked by more than a tradition of violent protest. All three areas faced agricultural depression and the fiscal pressures generated by the War of the Spanish Succession. Certain common economic denominators ran through all three insurrections. In Spain and France the peasants served as the locus of revolutionary activity—understandable in a society dominated by agriculture, a Malthusian society where population often outstripped the means of subsistence and where a rise in the price of bread sparked revolt. Throughout the Early Modern period, as the population began to rise, so too did the price of food. In 1500 Europe had approximately sixty-nine million people, in 1600 eighty-nine million, and by 1700, one hundred fifteen million. The price revolution of 1550 to 1650 only compounded the problem so that by the beginning of the eighteenth century the price of grain in Western Europe was nearly seven times higher than it had been in 1500. The price of other food products also rose, but real wages did not. The problem of subsistence dominated early-eighteenth-century society, a society poised between famine and plenty; a society, moreover, where the inelasticity of wages and the relative price rigidity of nonagricultural products aggravated the basic supply problem. Ninety percent of the population faced a lower standard of living and were worse off in 1715 than they had been in 1690. They lived in a world in which "technological backwardness had as much to do with the condition of the populace as exploitation by an oppressive ruling class."[26] The agricultural depression of the mid-seventeenth to the mid-eighteenth century explains in large part the unrest endemic among the peasantry throughout Europe. Agricultural poverty in Spain, France, and Hungary weakened the economy. Peasants in both France and Spain were poorer than their counterparts in both England and the United Provinces; they were unable to supply themselves consistently with the minimal needs of life. Deserted villages, empty farms, and neglected fields paint the same dismal picture of rural indebtedness and depopulation, a picture outlined by little reclamation activity, few agricultural innovations, and falling cereal prices. After 1650 cereal prices fell to one-third or one-fourth of their former value throughout most of Europe.[27] Fluctuations in grain prices and an unfavorable ratio between the price of grain and other commodities and wages characterized this and other agricultural recessions. In Valencia, using the years 1726–1750 = 100 as a base, real wages rose from 88.2 in 1656–1660 to 106.3 in 1701–1705 while the price of grain fell from 103.5 in 1656–1660 to 82.9 in 1671–1675 rising to 89.0 in 1701–1705.[28]

Throughout France too the period from 1687 to 1715 was generally one of low agricultural yields. Particularly in the south, Languedoc, Provence, Dauphiné, serious food shortages persisted in the 1680s and after. Nonetheless, cereal prices declined from 1662 until the mid–1680s and then stabilized. Using 1626 as the base year, wheat prices fell from 100 in 1626 to 59 in 1680–1690. After a short rise in 1680–1690, they continued to drop to 50 by 1750. Rent levels fell downward from the 1670s to the 1720s, reflecting the depreciation of the land. Land prices sank from 260 francs per hectare in the period from 1651 to 1675 to 175 in the period from 1701 to 1725, falling in some areas by as much as 80 percent. Wages, however, increased over the whole period, as did taxes. Most of the burden of these taxes, which increased enormously in France in the period from 1689 to 1713 and which absorbed as much as

15 percent of the national income, fell on the rural poor and the peasantry. Although it is true that taxes had risen faster in the period 1610–1660, proportionately the burden was heavier in the last part of the century because the ratio of taxes to yield had risen. The state, instead of ameliorating, only exacerbated the subsistence crisis. The peasant faced greater demands on dwindling resources.

The Little Ice Age, which gripped Europe from the 1550s to 1700, underlay the basic subsistence problem of the old regime.[29] "Everything moved to its rhythm." The 1690s were the coldest decade in seven hundred years.[30] Unusually severe winters recurred all too often throughout this period. Appreciably lower rainfall in both winter and spring and greater precipitation in summer lowered yields. Most of France suffered from wet and cold weather, while certain regions of Castile and Aragon and southern France faced hot and dry periods. Western Europe and the Mediterranean are climatological opposites; in the Mediterranean wet years produced good harvests, but in Western Europe wet years yielded poor crops. In certain areas of Castile and Aragon, for example, the shortage of spring rainfall proved critical. But in Spain and France the results were the same—low yields, which forced farmers to borrow disastrously and to turn to viticulture, as in Catalonia, or to husbandry or rural industry, especially textiles, as in France. In Languedoc, where the peasants had cultivated the olive, the severe frost of 1690 to 1700 damaged the trees. Languedoc, one of the most prosperous and commercially advanced parts of France, also had the largest textile industry, which employed about one-seventh of the provincial population by the middle of the eighteenth century. Unfortunately, these workers earned about one-third less than their counterparts did in England and the United Provinces. The industry itself did not recover from the textile slump following the revocation of the Edict of Nantes until 1708 or 1710. The wartime blockade and the increased competition from the English and the Dutch, particularly in the Levant, caused violent fluctuations in the export trade, further impoverishing France.[31]

In Hungary, where the evidence is more fragmentary, the same pattern persists, one of rural poverty. In spite of its different features, the Hungarian economy experienced the same crises and booms as that of Western Europe.[32] The predominance of Western Europe had turned East Central Europe into an economic backwater, a source of raw materials for Western Europe. At this time the share of Central Europe in international trade was declining. A strong bourgeoisie did not exist in Hungary. The middle class that did exist derived their incomes from trading in cattle, wine, and to some extent, corn. Although new crops such as maize and tobacco were introduced, there had been little innovation since the Middle Ages. The yield from crops was very low, similar to that in Poland and Slovakia. In a society dominated by agriculture, yield was crucial, for a fall in yield affected not only the individual farmer but the entire area. The decline in yield ratios throughout Central and Eastern Europe at this time was partially attributable to low cereal prices, which discouraged farmers from spending their time or money on the growing of cereal crops. Thus farmers tilled less land and turned instead to animal husbandry or viticulture. Andras Szirmay, for example, a member of an old, illustrious noble family and an adherent of Rákóczi, derived most of his income not from farming but from viticulture. His income from viticulture far exceeded that from tillage and animal husbandry. Those who did till the land often planted hops and tobacco instead of cereal crops. In both Royal and Ottoman Hungary, the lot of the peasant had deteriorated in the late seventeenth century.[33] In Ottoman Hungary the government forced the Christian peasants to pay a higher tax than their Muslim counterparts, consciously discriminating against those who "remained Christian, alien in language and culture as well as in religion."[34] The Habsburgs with their extensive geopolitical responsibilities were forced to raise taxes even higher than their European counterparts, such as the Bourbons, to offset their increased spending to pay off the governmental debt, which had tripled between 1700 and 1720. In 1698, for example, the Habsburgs doubled the contribution levied in Hungary. In spite of such measures Leopold faced a chronic deficit, a budgetary impasse he was unable to overcome in part because of the weakness of the economy and in part because of the dominance of the nobility, who limited the fiscal exactions of the state. Throughout Hungary the resulting high taxes led to deserted lands and endemic banditry. Understandably, economic grievances played a significant role in triggering unrest.[35]

Third, in all three revolts autonomous organizations threatened the centralized state. The Camisard revolt fits the passive typology of autonomy: the Camisards wanted to be left alone to practice their religion, while the Hungarians and the Spanish fall under the active typology, for they wanted a certain measure of independence from the central government. In France the Huguenot communities became independent foci of "social orientation and political loyalties," independent forces in society not only because of their separate organizational identity but also because of their value systems.[36] The Huguenots had an independent ideological system, a system that shaped the world according to a given set of values. The Camisards, living in a Bible-based culture, were oblivious of the secular values that buttressed the absolute state. Faced with the destruction of the local community and their way of life, they fought back desperately, even appealing to France's enemies, the Protestant powers of England and the United Provinces, for help. The author of a pamphlet aptly entitled *The Cevenois Reliev'd or else Europe Enslav'd* argued that the insurrection was lawful and that England should intervene.[37] The very existence of the Huguenots, then, threatened the basis of the absolute state. Identification with religious activity often meant loyalty to transcendental values rather than to a political community. The meaningful distinction was between the elect and the unregenerate, not the native and the foreigner. The fellowship of the church extended across borders. "We are," as one Huguenot supporter wrote, "in the same body, that of Christ." The group referent of the Huguenots, wider than that of territorial France, extended to Calvinists and even to other Protestants throughout Europe. After their defeat, many joined Louis's enemies and fought against France.[38] In 1706 the Huguenot churches in London issued a formal declaration of support for the conduct of the war against France. Pierre Jurieu became a paid informant of the English and actively assisted allied agents. Because their main referent was the religious, not the political, community, even those who did not actively join the rebellion hid and aided the rebels in the Cévennes.[39] The possibility that the Huguenots would actively or passively undermine the absolute state troubled rulers like Louis XIV, who did not want independent sources of power within France and who consciously tried to limit their development.

In a state where religious authority seconded in a certain measure the civil power, where the legitimation of the ruler was couched in religious terms, dissent could only be viewed as potentially if not actually seditious. The Huguenots, therefore, represented a very real threat in a state validated by religious sanctions, a theocratic state where God sanctified not only the king but the social order as well. The authorities could not but view Protestantism as a source of division, of rebellion.[40] The revolt had confirmed many in their belief that Protestantism should be equated with sedition and disorder. Even after the rebellion was suppressed, the persecution continued, but not with the same intensity. Only the fear of igniting another war dissuaded the authorities from harsher measures. The government did not succeed in extirpating Calvinism from the Cévennes. Prophetism continued as late as 1723 with the multipliants, a sect more and more removed from orthodox Calvinism. In 1762 the last pastor was executed and the last Camisard condemned to the galleys. It was not until 1768 that one of the prophetesses, Marie Durand, was freed and not until 1775 that those condemned to the galleys were released.

Just as Louis XIV had sought to destroy the power of the Protestants, so too did Leopold. The Hungarian Protestants had a larger frame of reference than just the state and appealed to other Protestant powers for aid just as their co-religionists in France had. The emperor sought not only to eradicate Protestantism but also to weaken the power of the Hungarians by creating new administrative structures that were dependent on the emperor, not on traditional sources. Louis XIV attempted to undermine the group consciousness of the Protestants just as Leopold attempted to weaken that of the Hungarians. Both represented autonomous and hence threatening foci of power.

Spain furnishes yet another example, for in centralizing the state Philip moved to eliminate the power of the grandees and to destroy provincial identities by attacking the *fueros*. In Spain the sense of community consciousness manifested itself primarily in an abiding distrust of outsiders, particularly Frenchmen. The historical and linguistic differences between Castilian and Catalan reinforced the sense of a separate community and heightened the friction between the principality and the central government. The Bourbon regime threatened the historical identity, even the survival, of their community. Their frame of reference, the community, the *patria*, embodied their historical rights and liberties. The Catalans cried out in 1640, as they would do later, *Visca la terra*.[41] The Huguenot in France, the Catalan in Spain, the *kuruc* in Hungary—all threatened the monopolistic power of the absolute state. In the latter two instances the rebels wanted to maintain their political rights and administrative jurisdictions. Both demanded the legalization of that autonomy. The Aragonese wanted reaffirmation of their traditional *fueros* within the Spanish state, while the Hungarians wanted the establishment of a separate state as embodied in their formal dethronement of the Habsburgs. The *Gesamtstaat* had triumphed in France and in Spain but not, at least to the same degree, in the Danubian monarchy. Thus, in an important sense, though Rákóczi lost, he won as well. This was not true in either Aragon or France.

In Spain, Hungary, and France the insurgents defended the traditional communities against the incursions of the *Gesamtstaat*. In all three cases the periphery rose against the center. Remote areas like Languedoc could shelter alternative forms of Christianity, which in turn checked the development of the royal state. Resistance to centralization was often allied with religious dissidence. Anomalous in many ways, the Camisard rebellion nonetheless provides a glimpse of the reactions of ordinary people to the encroachment of the state. The Camisard revolt represents for Tilly the "last great old regime rebellion," for thereafter "resistance to the state's expansion fragmented and declined." The future rebel would fight within "the perimeter of a well-established state."[42] As traditional societies, resisting disruption, none had a vision of or a striving for what could be called a revolutionary society. The use of the term *revolution* merely evokes certain anachronistic perceptions that cannot but obscure the nature of revolt in early modern Europe. The revolts were triggered in Spain and in Hungary by the fiscal pressures of war and by the diversions and the problems that war entailed. In France economic conditions exacerbated an already tense situation. As the military expenditures rose to 80 percent of the total expenses in France, taxes, already seen as a direct incursion of the state, increased. The ensuing pressure of taxes broke the traditional bonds. The economic crisis worsened the situation because it disrupted the social basis of a kingship society. What precipitated revolt was the centralization of state power and the attack on the local privileges and liberties that it necessitated. The cleavages of the early modern European world, whether national, ethnic, or religious, helped to ignite the insurrections. The tradition of violence and the identification with a certain community rather than the dynastic state both legitimized and fanned the ensuing violence. By containing the revolts the governments could eventually crush them.

The rebellions in Spain and Hungary flared up during the War of the Spanish Succession (1702–1714) in response to the tensions of a society at war and the fiscal burdens that war entailed. In all three instances the struggles were responses to the building of *Gesamtstaat*, the encroachment of the *Staat* at the expense of the *Stände*. In France, the revolt can be understood only as the clash of "two radically different cultural universes."[43] Although none were jacqueries, the revolts harnessed the energies of the most exploited order, the peasantry. In these three societies the gulf between the propertied and the propertyless had widened; the inflationary spiral, dubbed the price revolution, coupled with technological backwardness worsened the plight of the peasant. Peasant unrest was as old as the servile order and indeed an integral part of that order. Traditionally such violent protest was directed against concrete targets, especially those outside the community. These revolts followed that tradition. None attempted or even envisaged altering the aristocratic framework of the state, but their similarities and even their differences will reveal much about the extent of disaffection in early modern Europe and the response of the absolute state to unrest.[44] The insurrections illustrate the specificity of historical events and the difficulties of fitting them into an abstract system or specific typology. The revolts were local and historically conditioned reactions to and manifestations of great social dislocation.

Nonetheless, a study of these revolts, which were in large part peasant uprisings, may provide insight into both earlier and later conflicts. Undoubtedly these revolts are more similar to medieval insurrections than to modern revolutions. The Camisard revolt vividly illustrates—if one needs reminding—the tragic consequences of forced deculturation. In another context, another era, another continent, Jean-Paul Sartre would criticize the French in

Algeria for "wiping out their traditions, for substituting our language for theirs, and destroying their culture without giving them ours."[45] These revolts also address another problem, modernization in some contemporary societies. Some sociologists such as S. N. Eisenstadt have argued that "the transformation of the fundamental premises of the social and cultural order" and a "restructuring of the relationship between the center and the periphery" have meant that modern patterns of change represent a distinct break with traditional ones. By this logic of "an unbridgeable gap," change in modern society cannot be explained by any developments that occurred in traditional societies.[46] One cannot but heed Charles Tilly's warning about elevating "the idea of modernization into a model of change" and about making faulty implicit comparison between today's Third World and yesterday's Europe."[47] Indeed, the inexorability of a modernization or underdevelopment model, besides introducing a certain teleology, tends to obscure the differences between countries and time periods.[48] These problems, obvious enough in relation to twentieth-century questions, become overwhelming when projected back into the eighteenth century. Yet these early modern societies, like various modern ones, were being "detraditionalized,"[49] increasingly integrated into larger economic and political networks. These rebellions enable us to freeze a moment in time, a moment when people fought against the implacable growth of the state. The central government extended its legal, administrative, economic, and political activities. The local community fought back with tragic consequences. It was a fight they could not win.

NOTES

1. Ted Gurr, *Why Men Rebel* (Princeton, N.J., 1970), p. 171.
2. J. H. Elliott, "Revolts in the Spanish Monarchy," in *Preconditions of Revolution in Early Modern Europe*, edited by Robert Forster and Jack P. Greene (Baltimore, 1970), p. 110.
3. Roland Mousnier, *Peasant Uprisings in Seventeenth-Century France, Russia, and China* (New York, 1970), p. 329.
4. Charles Tilly, *The Contentious French* (Cambridge, Mass., 1986), pp. 139 and 155.
5. Tilly contends that by the end of the seventeeth century "the seizure

of grain displaced tax rebellions as the most frequent occasion" of collective action. Ibid., p. 156.

6. Jean Cavalier, *Mémoires sur la guerre des Camisards*, annotated by Frank Puaux (Paris, 1979), p. 24.

7. Ibid., p. 58.

8. G. Paysan, *Les Camisards du Vivarais* (Le Mazel Banne, 1981), p. 132.

9. Henry Marczali, *Hungary in the Eighteenth Century* (Cambridge, 1910), p. lii. Also see Orest Subtelny, *Domination of Eastern Europe: Native Nobilities and Foreign Absolutism, 1500–1715* (Montreal, 1986), pp. 75–85.

10. Tezner, quoted in Zoltan Kramer, "The Military Ethos of the Hungarian Nobility, 1700–1848," *Special Topics and Generalizations on the 18th and 19th Centuries*, pp. 67 and 79; László Benczédi, "The Warrior Estate in the 17th Century with Special Reference to the Thokoly Uprising (1678–1685)," in *From Hunyadi to Rákóczi: War and Society in Late Medieval and Early Modern Hungary*, edited by Janos M. Bak and Béla K. Király (New York, 1982), pp. 351–365, and Bela K. Kiraly, "Society and War from Mounted Knights to the Standing Armies of Absolute Kings," in *From Hunyadi to Rákóczi*, p. 26.

11. Henry Kamen, *Spain, 1469–1714, A Society of Conflict* (New York, 1983), pp. 240–241; and Kamen, *Spain in the Late Seventeenth Century* (New York, 1980), pp. 175–182.

12. John Lynch, *Spain under the Habsburgs* (New York, 1964), 1:337. Also see pp. 338–345 and Kamen, *Spain, 1469–1714*, pp. 139–144.

13. J. H. Elliott, *The Revolt of the Catalans: A Study in the Decline of Spain* (Cambridge, 1963), p. 375.

14. Lynch, *Spain*, 2:101; also see pp. 102–107.

15. Elliott, "Revolts in the Spanish Monarchy," p. 114. Also see Perez Zagorin, *Rebels and Rulers, 1500–1660* (Cambridge, 1982), 2:32–37.

16. Kamen, *Spain, 1469–1714*, p. 237. Also see Pierre Vilar, *La Catalogne dans l'Espagne moderne: Recherches sur les fondements economiques des structurales nationales* (Paris, 1962), pp. 676–678.

17. Quoted in Elliott, "Revolts in the Spanish Monarchy," p. 112.

18. Kamen, *Spain, 1469–1714*, p. 214. Also see pp. 212–219.

19. Ibid., p. 218.

20. Henry Kamen, "A Forgotten Insurrection of the Seventeenth Century: The Catalan Peasant Rising of 1688," *Journal of Modern History* 49 (June 1977), pp. 210–130.

21. Kamen, *Spain, 1469–1714*, pp. 212–221 and Lynch, *Spain*, 2:256–259.

22. Eric Hobsbawn, *Bandits* (New York, 1981), p. 23.

23. Ibid., p. 178.

24. Agnes R. Varkonyi, "Politique envers les serfs et developpement culturel dans l'état du Rákóczi." *Acta Historica* 27 (1981):31.

25. James Fenimore Cooper, quoted in Hannah Arendt, *On Revolution* (New York, 1963), pp. 141–142.

26. J. H. Elliott, "Revolution and Continuity in Early Modern Europe." *Past and Present* 42 (February 1969):45.

27. Francois Simiand, *Recherches anciennes et nouvelles sur le mouvement general des prix du XVI au XIX siecle* (Paris, 1932), passim.

28. Kamen, *Spain, 1469–1714*, p. 104.

29. For another view of the role of climate see Emmanuel Le Roy Ladurie, "Historie et climat," *Annales: Économies, sociétés, civilisations* 14 (1959):3–34.

30. Fernand Braudel, *Civilization and Capitalism, 15th to 18th Century*, vol.I: *The Limits of the Possible* (New York, 1979), p. 49.

31. Wilhelm Abel, *Agricultural Fluctuations in Europe from the 13th to the 20th Centuries* (London, 1978), pp. 158–173; B. H. Slicher van Bath, *The Agrarian History of Western Europe* A.D. *500–1850* (London, 1963), pp. 206–219; B. H. Slicher van Bath, "Agriculture in the Vital Revolution," *The Cambridge Economic History* 5(1977):42–71; Ralph Davis, *The Rise of the Atlantic Economies* (Ithaca, N.Y., 1973), pp. 122–124, 216–229; Tihomir J. Markovitch, *Les Industries lainières de Colbert à la Revolution* (Geneva, 1976), pp. 271–310; J. K. J. Thomson, *Clermont-de-Lodeve, 1633–1789* (Cambridge, 1982), passim; Georges d'Avenel, *Histoire économique de la propriété, des salaires, des denrées et de tous les prix en général depuis l'an 1200 jusqu'en l'an 1800* (Paris, 1894–1905), vols. 1 and 3, passim.

32. F. Szakály, "Hungary and Eastern Europe," *Études historiques hongroises* 2 (1980):660.

33. Ágnes R. Várkonyi, "Husbandry among the Nobility of Hungary at the Turn of the 18th Century: Their Mentality and Some Problems of Long-Range Socio-Historical Development," *Acta Historico-Oeconomica Iugosloviae* 9(1982):75–96; Leonid Zytkowicz, "Grain Yields in Poland, Hungary and Slovakia in the 16th to 18th Centuries," *Acta Poloniae Historica* 24 (1971):51–72; B. H. Slicher van Bath, "The Yields of Different Crops (Mainly in Relation to the Seed, c. 810–1820)," *Acta Historica Neerlandica* 2(1967):26–106.

34. Wayne Vucinich, "The Nature of Balkan Society under Ottoman Rule," *Slavic Review* 21 (December 1962):597–616; also refer to Ilber Ortayli, "The Late Seventeenth Century Ottoman Empire," paper delivered at Conference on the Ottoman and Habsburg Empires during the Second Half of the Seventeenth Century, 17–19 October 1983, Bloomington, Indiana.

35. Jean Berenger, *Finances et absolutisme autrichien dans la seconde moitié du XVII siècle* (Paris, 1975); and Jim Riley, "Austrian Finances during the Seventeenth Century," paper delivered at Conference on Ottoman and Habsburg Empires.

36. For a general discussion of this question see S. N. Eisenstadt, *The Political Systems of Empires* (London, 1963), pp. 62–64 and 140–191.

37. *The Cevenois Reliev'd or else Europe Enslav'd* (London, 1703).

38. B.M., Add. Mss. 61,258 fols. 203–205, is a memorial from a number of Huguenots who served Louis, deserted, and who now want to return to help their brethren. This bundle contains letters from Cavalier to Marlborough concerning various military projects and their costs. One such project envisioned sending 12 companies of 66 men each to Catalonia (fol. 125). Also see fol. 27, which contains a memorial of 3 November 1710 addressed to the queen.

39. For the basic autonomy of religious organizations see S. N. Eisenstadt, *Tradition, Change and Modernity* (New York, 1973), p. 193.

40. Ernest Albaric, *Essai sur l'ésprit national du protestantisme francaise au XVIe et au XVIIe siecle* (1853; reprint Geneva, 1969), pp. 2–3; and Gabriel Lebras, *Etudes de sociologie religieuse* (New York, 1975).

41. Elliott, "Revolution and Continuity," p. 48.

42. Tilly, *The Contentious French*, pp. 176 and 199.

43. Philippe Joutard, *La Legende des Camisards: Une Sensibilite au passé* (Paris, 1977), p. 39.

44. Porshnev linked peasant uprisings with the development of the early modern state. Winfried Schulze, "Peasant Resistance in Sixteenth- and Seventeenth-Century Germany in a European Context," in *Religion, Politics, and Social Protest: Three Studies in Early Modern Germany*, edited by Kaspar von Greyerz, p. 65.

45. Franz Fanon, *The Wretched of the Earth* (New York, 1966), p. 13.

46. Gary G. Hamilton, "Configurations in History: The Historical Sociology of S. N. Eisenstadt," in *Vision and Method in Historical Sociology*, edited by Theda Skocpol, p. 91.

47. Quoted in Lynn Hunt, "Charles Tilly's Collective Action," in *Vision and Method in Historical Sociology*, p. 247.

48. See Theda Skocpol and Michael Burawoy, eds., *Marxist Inquiries: Studies of Labor, Class, and States* (Chicago, 1982), p. S20.

49. S. N. Eisenstadt, "Breakdowns of Modernization," *Economic Development and Cultural Change* 12 (July 1964):346.

A Select Bibliography of Printed Sources

GENERAL AND THEORETICAL WORKS

Arendt, Hannah. *On Revolution*. New York, 1963
———. *On Violence*. New York, 1969.
Bak, János, and Benecke, Gerhard, eds. *Religion and Rural Revolt*. Manchester, 1984.
Bassiouni, M. Cherif, ed. *International Terrorism and Political Crimes*. Springfield, Ill., 1975.
Bell, J. Bowyer. *On Revolt: Strategies of National Liberation*. Cambridge, Mass., 1976.
Blackey, Robert, and Payne, Clifford T., eds. *Why Revolution? Theories and Analyses*. Cambridge, Mass., 1971.
Blum, Jerome. *The End of the Old Order in Rural Europe*. Princeton, N. J., 1978.
Burke, Peter. "Mediterranean Europe 1500–1800: Notes and Comparisons." In *Religion and Rural Revolt*, edited by János Bak and Gerhard Benecke, pp. 75–85. Manchester, 1984.
———. *Popular Culture in Early Modern Europe*. New York, 1978.
Clutterbuck, Richard L. *Guerrillas and Terrorists*. Athens, Ga., 1977.
Cohn, Norman. *The Pursuit of the Millennium*. London, 1957.
Davies, James C. "Toward a Theory of Revolution." *American Sociological Review* 27 (February 1962):5–19.
Davis, Ralph. *The Rise of the Atlantic Economies*. Ithaca, N.Y., 1973.

Eckstein, Harry. "On the Etiology of Internal War." *History and Theory* 4 (1965):133–163.
Eisenstadt, S. N. "Breakdowns of Modernization." *Economic Development and Cultural Change* 12 (July 1964):345–367.
———. *Modernization: Protest and Change*. Englewood Cliffs, N.J., 1966.
———. *The Political Systems of Empires*. London, 1963.
———. *Revolution and the Transformation of Societies: A Comparative Study of Civilizations*. New York, 1978.
———. *Tradition, Change and Modernity*. New York, 1973.
Elliott, J. H. "Revolution and Continuity in Early Modern Europe." *Past and Present* 42 (February 1969):35–56.
Etzioni, Amitai, and Etzioni-Halevy, Eva. *Social Change: Sources, Patterns, and Consequences*. New York, 1973.
Evans, Peter B.; Rueschemeyer, Dietrich; and Skocpol, Theda, eds. *Bringing the State Back In*. Cambridge, 1985.
Forster, Robert, and Greene, Jack P., eds. *Preconditions of Revolution in Early Modern Europe*. Baltimore, 1971.
Gann, Lewis H. *Guerrillas in History*. Stanford, Calif., 1971.
Griewank, Karl. *Die neuzeitliche Revolutionsbegriff*. Weimar, 1955.
Gurr, Ted. *Why Men Rebel*. Princeton, N.J., 1970.
Hamilton, Gary G. "Configurations in History: The Historical Sociology of S. N. Eisenstadt." In *Vision and Method in Historical Sociology*, edited by Theda Skocpol, pp. 85–128. Cambridge, 1984.
Hoare, Quintin, and Smith, Geoffrey Nowell, eds. and trans. *Selections from the Prison Notebooks of Antonio Gramsci*. London, 1971.
Hobsbawm, Eric. *Bandits*. New York, 1981.
———. *Primitive Rebels*. New York, 1959.
Hunt, Lynn. *Politics, Culture and Class in the French Revolution*. Berkeley, Calif., 1984.
———. "Charles Tilly's Collective Action." In *Vison and Method in Historical Sociology*, edited by Theda Skocpol, pp. 244–275. Cambridge, 1984.
Jessop, Bob. *Social Order, Reform and Revolution*. New York, 1972.
Johnson, Chalmers. *Revolution and the Social System*. Stanford, Calif., 1974.
———. *Revolutionary Change*. Stanford, Calif., 1982.
Koselleck, Reinhart. *Futures Past: On the Semantics of Historical Time*. Cambridge, Mass., 1985.
Landsberger, Henry A., ed. *Rural Protest: Peasant Movements and Social Change*. New York, 1973.
Laqueur, Walter. *Guerrilla: A Historical and Critical Study*. Boston, 1976.
———. *Terrorism*. Boston, 1977.

Lewy, Guenther. *Religion and Revolution*. New York, 1974.
Mallison, W. T., and Mallison, S. V. "The Concept of Public Purpose Terror in International Law: Doctrines and Sanctions to Reduce the Destruction of Human and Material Values." In *International Terrorism and Political Crimes*, edited by M. Cherif Bassiouni, pp. 67–85. Springfield, Ill., 1975.
Mannheim, Karl. *Essays on the Sociology of Culture*. London, 1956.
———. *Ideology and Utopia: An Introduction to the Sociology of Knowledge*. New York, 1936.
Marx, Karl, and Engels, Friedrich. *Manifesto of the Communist Party*. New York, 1932.
Merriman, Roger Bigelow. *Six Contemporaneous Revolutions*. Hamden, Conn., 1963.
Moore, Barrington. *Injustice: The Social Bases of Obedience and Revolt*. White Plains, N.Y., 1978.
Moote, A. Lloyd. "The Preconditions of Revolution in Early Modern Europe: Did They Really Exist?" *Canadian Journal of History* 7 (December 1972):207–234.
Mousnier, Roland. *Peasant Uprisings in Seventeenth-Century France, Russia, and China*. New York, 1970.
Parsons, Talcott, ed. *Toward a General Theory of Action*. Cambridge, Mass., 1951.
Rabb, Theodore K. *The Struggle for Stability in Early Modern Europe*. New York, 1975.
Rudé, George. *Ideology and Popular Protest*. New York, 1980.
Schulze, Winfried. "Peasant Resistance in Sixteenth- and Seventeenth-Century Germany in a European Context." In *Religion, Politics, and Social Protest: Three Studies in Early Modern Germany*, edited by Kaspar von Greyerz, pp. 61–98. London, 1984.
Scott, Tom. "Peasant Revolts in Early Modern Germany." *The Historical Journal* 28 (June 1985):455–468.
Skocpol, Theda. *States and Social Revolutions: A Comparative Analysis of France, Russia, and China*. Cambridge, 1979.
———, ed. *Vision and Method in Historical Sociology*. Cambridge, 1984.
———, and Burawoy, Michael, eds. *Marxist Inquiries: Studies of Labor, Class, and States*. Chicago, 1982.
Sorokin, Pitirim A. *Social and Cultural Dynamics*. New York, 1937.
Stone, Lawrence. "Theories of Revolution." *World Politics* 18 (January 1966):159–176.
Tilly, Charles. *From Mobilization to Revolution*. Reading, Mass., 1978.
———. "War Making and State Making as Organized Crime." In *Bringing the State Back In*, edited by Peter B. Evans, Dietrich Rueschemeyer, and Theda Skocpol, pp. 169–191. Cambridge, 1985.

Tocqueville, Alexis de. *The Ancien Régime and the French Revolution*. New York, 1955.
Wilkinson, Paul. *Political Terrorism*. London, 1974.
Zagorin, Perez. *Rebels and Rules, 1500–1660*. Cambridge, 1982.
———. "Theories of Revolution in Contemporary Historiography." *Political Science Quarterly* 87 (March 1973):23–52.

FRANCE

Albaric, Ernst. *Essai sur l'esprit national du protestantisme français au XVIe et au XVIIe siècle*. 1853. Reprint Geneva, 1969.
Almeras, Charles. *La Révolte des Camisards*. Paris, 1959.
Armogathe, Jean-Robert, and Joutard, Philippe. "Bâville et la guerre des Camisards." *Revue d'histoire moderne et contemporaine* 19 (1972):45–67.
Avenel, Georges vicomte d'. *Histoire économique de la propriété, des salaires, des denrées et de tous les prix en général depuis l'an 1200 jusqu'en l'an 1800*. Paris, 1894–1905.
Bâville, Nicolas Lamoignon de. *Mémoires pour servir à l'histoire de Languedoc*. Amsterdam, 1734.
Blanc, Hippolyte. *De l'inspiration des Camisards*. 1859. Reprint Provence, 1978.
Boislisle, George Michel de, ed. *Mémoires de Saint-Simon*. Paris, 1928.
Boissonade, P. "La Production et le commerce des céréales, des vins et des eaux-de-vie." *Annales du Midi* 17 (1905):329–360.
Bonbonnoux, Jacques. *Mémoires de Bonbonnoux, chef Camisard et pasteur du désert*. Cévennes, 1883.
Briggs, Robin. *Early Modern France, 1560–1715*. New York, 1977.
Cavalier, Jean. *Mémoires sur la guerre des Camisards*. Paris, 1973. [Edition of 1979 edited by Frank Puaux.]
Chamson, André. *Catinat, gardian de la Camargue, chef de la cavalerie camisarde*. Paris, 1983.
———. *Castanet, le Camisard de l'Aigoual*. Paris, 1979.
Court, Antoine. *Histoire des troubles des Cévennes ou de la guerre des Camisards sous le règne de Louis le Grand*. 1760. Reprint Marseilles, 1975.
Dodge, Guy H. *The Political Theory of the Huguenots of the Dispersion with Special Reference to the Thought and Influence of Pierre Jurieu*. New York, 1947.
Ducasse, André. *La Guerre des Camisards: La Résistance huguenote sous Louis XIV*. Paris, 1962.
Dumas, André. *Le Désert cévenol*. Paris, 1932.

Gagg, Robert P. *Das Leben der südfranzösischen Hugenottenkirche nach dem Todesurteil durch Ludwig XIV*. Zurich, 1961.

Garrisson-Estebe, Janine. *L'Homme protestante*. Paris, 1980.

Gorce, Agnes de la. *Camisards et dragons du roi*. Paris, 1950.

Grubb, Arthur. *Jean Cavalier*. London 1931.

Guiscard, Marquis de. *Memoirs*. London, 1705.

Histoire des Camisards. London, 1754.

Jones, Peter. "Antoine de Guiscard, 'Abbé de la Bourlie,' 'Marquis de Guiscard,' " *British Library Journal* 8 (Spring 1982) 94–113.

Joutard, Philippe. "Les Camisards: Prophètes de la grande Révolution ou derniers combattants des guerres de religion?" In *L'Esprit républicain: Colloque d'Orleans, 4 et 5 septembre 1970*, edited by Jacques Viard, pp. 113–123. Paris, 1972.

———. *La Légende des Camisards: Une Sensibilité au passé*. Paris, 1977.

———, ed. *Les Camisards*. Paris, 1976.

———, ed. *Journaux Camisards (1700–1715)*. Paris, 1965.

Labrousse, Ernst, et al. *Histoire économique et sociale de la France*. Paris, 1970.

Le Roy Ladurie, Emmanuel. *The Peasants of Languedoc*. Chicago, 1974.

Markovitch, Tihomir J. *Les industries lainières de Colbert à la Révolution*. Geneva, 1976.

Mazel, Abraham. *Mémoires inédit d'Abraham Mazel et d'Élie Marion sur la guerre des Cévennes, 1701–1708*. Vol. 34 of *The Publications of the Huguenot Society of London*. Paris, 1931.

Meuvret, Jean. *Le Problème des subsistances à l'époque Louis XIV: La Production des céréales dans la France du XVIIe et du XVIIIe siècle*. Paris, 1977.

Miquel, Pierre. *Les Guerres de religion*. Paris, 1980.

Misson, Maximilien. *Le Théâtre sacré des Cévennes*. Marseilles, 1977.

Mousnier, Roland. *Peasant Uprisings in Seventeenth-Century France, Russia, and China*. New York, 1970.

Paysan, G. *Les Camisards du Vivarais*. Le Mazel–Banne, 1981.

Pezet, Maurice. *L'Épopée des Camisards, Languedoc, Vivarais, Cévennes*. Paris, 1978.

Pillorget, René. *Les Mouvements insurrectionels de Provence*. Paris, 1975.

Porshnev, Boris Fedorovich. *Les Soulèvements populaires en France de 1623 à 1648*. Paris, 1963.

Précis historique de la guerre des Camisards, 1702–1710. Nimes, 1892.

Schwartz, Hillel. *The French Prophets: The History of a Millenarian Group in Eighteenth-Century England*. Berkeley, Calif., 1980.

———. *Knaves, Fools, Madmen, and That Subtle Effluvium: A Study of the Opposition to the French Prophets in England, 1706–1711*. Gainesville, Fl., 1978.

Simiand, François. *Recherches anciennes et nouvelles sur le mouvement général des prix du XVIe au XIXe siècle.* Paris, 1932.
Vidal, Daniel. *L'ablatif absolu, théorie du prophetisme, le discours camisard en Europe (1706–1713).* Paris, 1977.
Villenoisy, H. de. "L'Abbé du Cherla, monstre sadistique ou martyr de la foi." *Almanach cevenol* 5:73–87.

HUNGARY

Archivum Rákóczianum. 15 vols. Budapest, 1873–1889, 1935, 1955–1961, 1978.
Benczédi, László. "The Warrior Estate in the 17th Century with Special Reference to the Thököly Uprising (1678–1685)." In *War and Society in Eastern Central Europe.* vol. 3: *From Hunyadi to Rákóczi: War and Society in Late Medieval and Early Modern Hungary*, edited by János M. Bak and Béla K. Király, pp. 351–365. New York, 1982.
Benda, Kálmán. "Le Projet d'alliance hungaro-suedo-prussienne de 1704." *Études Historiques* 1 (1960):669–694.
———. "The Rákóczi War of Independence and the European Powers." In *War and Society in Eastern Central Europe*, vol. 3: *From Hunyadi to Rákóczi: War and Society in Late Medieval and Early Modern Hungary*, edited by János M. Bak and Béla K. Király, pp. 433–444. New York, 1982.
———. "Der Rákóczi-Aufstand in Ungarn und die europäischen Mächte (1703–1711)." *Österreich in Geschichte und Literatur* 22 (1978):328–337.
———, ed. *Europa es a Rákóczi-szabadságharac.* Budapest, 1980.
———; Esze, Tamás; Maksay, Ferenc; and Pap, Laszlo, ed. *Ráday Pál Iratai, 1703–1706.* Budapest, 1955.
Benda, Kálmán and Maksay, Ferenc, ed. *Ráday Pál Iratia, 1707–1708.* Budapest, 1961.
Berenger, Jean. *Finances et absolutisme autrichien dans la seconde moitié du XVII siècle.* Paris, 1975.
Boislisle, George Michel de, ed. *Mémoires de Saint-Simon.* Vol. 5. Paris, 1928.
Brenner, Domokos. *Histoire des révolutions de Hongrie.* The Hague, 1739.
Broucek, Peter. "The Border Defenses of Lower Austria, Styria, and Moravia against the Turks and Rákóczi's Insurgents." In *War and Society in Eastern Central Europe.* vol. 3: *From Hunyadi to Rákóczi: War and Society in Eastern Central Europe*, edited by János M. Bak and Béla K. Király, pp. 493–513. New York, 1982.

Bucsay, Mihály. *Der Protestantismus in Ungarn, 1521–1978.* Vienna, 1977.
Eszlary, Charles d'. "La Situation des serfs en Hongrie de 1514 à 1848." *Revue d'histoire économique et sociale* 38 (1961):385–417.
Frey, Linda, and Frey, Marsha. "Insurgency during the War of the Spanish Succession: The Rákóczi Revolt." *American Historical Association Proceedings* (1982). Also in *Hungarian Studies* 1 (1985):191–201.
———. "The Rákóczi Insurrection and the Disruption of the Grand Alliance." *Canadian-American Review of Hungarian Studies* 5 (Fall 1978):17–29.
———. "Rákóczi and the Maritime Powers: An Uncertain Friendship." In *War and Society in Eastern Central Europe,* vol. 3: *From Hunyadi to Rákóczi: War and Society in Late Medieval and Early Modern Hungary,* edited by János M. Bak and Béla K. Király, pp. 455–466. New York, 1982.
———. "II. Rákóczi Ferenc es a tengeri hátalmak." *Történelmi Szemle* (June 1982):663–674.
Grunwald, Max. *Samuel Oppenheimer und sein Kreis: Ein Kapitel aus der Finanzgeschichte Österreichs.* Vienna, 1913.
Hammerl, P. Benedict. "Die Einfälle der Kuruczen in die Gegend an der March in den Jahren 1703–1706." *Blätter des Vereins für Landeskunde von Niederösterreich* 24 (1890):284–301.
Hattendorf, John. "The Rákóczi Insurrection in English War Policy, 1703–1711." *Canadian-American Review of Hungarian Studies* 7 (Fall 1980):91–102.
Heckenast, Gustav. "Equipment and Supply of Ferenc II Rákóczi's Army." In *War and Society in Eastern Central Europe,* vol. 3: *From Hunyadi to Rákóczi: War and Society in Late Medieval and Early Modern Hungary,* edited by János M. Bak and Béla K. Király, pp. 421–431. New York, 1982.
Hengelmüller, Ladislas. *Hungary's Fight for National Existence.* London, 1913.
Horn, Émile. *François Rákóczy II, Prince de Transylvanie.* Paris, 1906.
Ingrao, Charles. "Guerrilla Warfare in Early Modern Europe. The *Kuruc* War (1703–1711)." In *War and Society in East Central Europe.* Vol. 1: *Special Topics and Generalizations on the Eighteenth and Nineteenth Centuries,* edited by Béla Király and Gunter E. Rothenberg, pp. 47–79. New York, 1979.
———. *In Quest and Crisis: Emperor Joseph I and the Habsburg Monarchy.* West Lafayette, Ind., 1979.
Joubert, Joseph. *François Rákóczy II, prince de Transylvanie.* Angiers, 1907.
Király, Béla K. *Hungary in the Late Eighteenth Century: The Decline of Enlightened Despotism.* New York, 1969.

———. "Society and War from Mounted Knights to the Standing Armies of Absolute Kings." In *War and Society in Eastern Central Europe*, vol. 3: *From Hunyadi to Rákóczi: War and Society in Late Medieval and Early Modern History.* edited by János M. Bak and Béla K. Király, pp. 23–55. New York, 1982.

———. "War and Society in Western and East Central Europe during the Eighteenth and Nineteenth Centuries: Similarities and Contrasts." In *War and Society in East Central Europe*, vol. 1: *Special Topics and Generalizations on the Eighteenth and Nineteenth Centuries*, edited by Béla K. Király and Gunther E. Rothenberg, pp. 1–33. New York, 1979.

———. "War and Society in Western and East Central Europe in the Pre-Revolutionary Eighteenth Century." In *War and Society in Eastern Central Europe*, vol. 2: *East Central European Society and War in the Pre-Revolutionary Eighteenth Century*, edited by Gunther E. Rothenberg, Béla K. Király, and Peter F. Sugar, pp. 1–25. New York, 1982.

Kirilly, Zs.; Makkai, L.; Kiss, I. N.; and Zimányi, V. "Production et productivité agricoles en Hongrie à l'époque du féodalisme tardif (1550–1850)." *Nouvelles études historiques* 1(1965):581–638.

Klopp, Onno. *Der Fall des Hauses Stuart.* Vienna, 1879.

Köpeczi, Béla. *L'Autobiographie d'un prince rebelle: Confession et mémoires de François II Rákóczi* Budapest, 1977.

———. "La Guerre d'indépendance hongroise au début du XVIII siècle et l'Europe." *Acta Historica Academiae Scientiarum Hungaricae* 22 (1976):331–341.

———. "The Hungarian Wars of Independence of the Seventeenth and Eighteenth Centuries in Their European Context." In *War and Society in Eastern Central Europe*, vol 3: *From Hunyadi to Rákóczi: War and Society in Late Medieval and Early Modern Hungary*, edited by János M. Bak and Béla K. Király, pp. 445–453. New York, 1982.

———. *La France et la Hongrie au début de XVIII siècle.* Budapest, 1971.

———; Hopp, Lajos; and Várkonyi, Ágnes, eds. *Rákóczi-Tanulmányok.* Budapest, 1980.

Köpeczi, Bela, and Várkonyi, Ágnes. *II Rákóczi Ferenc.* Budapest, 1976.

Kramar, Zoltan. "The Military Ethos of the Hungarian Nobility, 1700–1848." In *War and Society in Eastern Central Europe*, vol. 1: *Special Topics and Generalizations on the Eighteenth and Nineteenth Centuries*, edited by Béla Király and Gunther E. Rothenberg, pp. 67–79. New York, 1979.

Kurat, Akdes Nimet. *The Despatches of Sir Robert Sutton, Ambassador to Constantinople (1710–1714).* London, 1953.

Lefaivre, Albert. "L'Insurrection magyare sous François II Rágóczy, 1703–1711." *Revue des questions historiques* 25 (1901):518–586.

———. *Les Magyars pendant le domination ottomane en Hongrie, 1526–1721.* Paris, 1902.

Legrelle, Arsène. *La Diplomatie française et la succession d'Espagne.* Paris, 1892.

Makkai, Laszlo. "La Structure et la productivité de l'économie agraire de la hongrie au milieu du xviie siècle." *Spoteczenstwo Gospodarka Kultura* (1974):197–207.

Marczali, Henry. *Hungary in the Eighteenth Century.* Cambridge, 1910.

Mensi, Franz von. *Die Finanzen Oesterreichs von 1701 bis 1740.* Vienna, 1890.

Pach, P. Zs. "The Diminishing Share of East-Central Europe in the 17th Century International Trade." *Acta Historica Academiae Scientiarum Hungaricae* 16 (1970):289–306.

———. "Le Problème du rassemblement des forces nationales pendant la guerre d'indépendance de François II Rákóczi." *Acta Historica* 3 (1956):95–113.

———. "The Shifting of International Trade Routes in the 15th–17th Centuries." *Acta Historica Academiae Scientiarum Hungaricae* 14 (1968):287–321.

Pastor, Peter. "Hungarian-Russian Relations during the Rákóczi War of Independence." In *War and Society in Eastern Central Europe*, vol. 3: *From Hunyadi to Rákóczi: War and Society in Late Medieval and Early Modern Hungary*, edited by János M. Bak and Béla K. Király, pp. 467–492. New York, 1982.

Perjés, Géza. "Army Provisioning, Logistics and Strategy in the Second Half of the 17th Century." *Acta Historica, Academiae Scientiarum Hungariacae* 16 (1970):1–52.

———. "Reflections on the Strategic Decisions of Ferenc II Rákóczi's War of Independence." In *War and Society in Eastern Central Europe*, vol. 3: *From Hunyadi to Rákóczi: War and Society in Late Medieval and Early Modern Hungary*, edited by János M. Bak and Béla K. Király, pp. 393–419.

Posch, Fritz. *Flammende Grenze: Die Steiermark in den Kuruzzensturmen.* Vienna, 1968.

Rákóczi II, Ferenc. *Histoire.* Cassovie, 1707.

———. *Histoire de révolution de Hongrie avec les mémoires.* The Hague, 1739.

———. *Mémoires du Prince François II Rákóczi sur la guerre de Hongrie depuis 1703 jusqu'a sa fin.* Budapest, 1978.

———. *Testament politique et moral.* The Hague, 1751.

Rázsó, Gy. "La Situation militaire générale et la guerre d'indépendance de Rákóczi." *Acta Historica Academiae Scientiarum Hungaricae* 22 (1976):367–375.
Savoy, Eugene of. *Feldzüge*. Vienna, 1876.
Spielman, John P. *Leopold I of Austria*. New Brunswick, N.J., 1977.
Subtelny, Orest. *Domination of Eastern Europe: Native Nobilities and Foreign Absolutism, 1500–1715*. Montreal, 1986.
Szakály, F., et al. "Hungary and Eastern Europe." *Études historiques hongroises* 2 (1980):613–805.
Várkonyi, Ágnes R. " 'Ad Pacem Universalem': The International Antecedents of the Peace of Szatmár." *Études historiques hongroises* 1 (1980):305–338.
———. "Évolution sociale et autonomie de l'État: (L'Absolutisme des Habsbourg et l'indépendance de la Hongrie)." *Acta Historica Academiae Scientiarum Hungaricae* 22 (1976):343–365.
———. "Hapsburg Absolutism and Serfdom in Hungary at the Turn of the 17th and 18th Centuries." *Nouvelle études historiques* 1 (1965):355–387.
———. "Husbandry among the Nobility of Hungary at the Turn of the 18th Century, Their Mentality, and Some Problems of Long-Range Socio-Historical Development." *Acta Historico-Oeconomica Iugoslaviae* 9 (1982):75–95.
———. "Politique envers les serfs et développement culturel dans l'état de Rákóczi." *Acta Historica* 27 (1981):31–61.
———. "Rákóczi's War of Independence and the Peasantry." In *War and Society in Eastern Central Europe*, vol. 3: *From Hunyadi to Rákóczi: War and Society in Late Medieval and Early Modern Hungary*, edited by Béla K. Király and János M. Bak, pp. 369–391. New York, 1982.
Várkonyi, Ágnes. "Repopulation and the System of Cultivation in Hungary after the Expulsion of the Turks." *Acta Historica Academiae Scientiarum Hungaricae* 16 (1970):151–170.
Vucinich, Wayne. "The Nature of Balkan Society under Ottoman Rule." *Slavic Review* 21 (December 1962):597–616.
Wessely, Kurt. "The Development of the Hungarian Military Frontier until the Middle of the Eighteenth Century." *Austrian History Yearbook* 9–10 (1973–1974):55–63.
Zimányi, Vera. "Mouvements des prix hongrois et l'évolution européenne (XVIe–XVIIIe s.)" *Acta Historica Academiae Scientiarum Hungaricae* 19 (1973):305–333.
———. "A Typology of Central European Inflation in the XVIth and XVIIth Centuries." *Journal of European Economic History* 4 (1975):399–402.

Zytkowicz, Leonid. "Grain Yields in Poland, Bohemia, Hungary, and Slovakia in the 16th to 18th Centuries." *Acta Poloniae Historica* 24 (1971):51–72.

SPAIN

Baudrillart, Alfred. *Philippe V et la cour de France, 1700–1715.* Paris, 1889.
Berwick, James Fitz-James, duke of. *Mémoires du maréchal de Berwick.* Switzerland, 1778 (English edition London, 1779.)
Caro Baroja, Julio. *Los moriscos del reino de Granada, ensayo de historia social.* Madrid, 1957.
Coxe, William. *Memoirs of the Kings of Spain of the House of Bourbon from the Accession of Philip V to the Death of Charles III, 1700–1788.* London, 1815.
Domínguez Ortiz, Antonio. *Sociedad y estado en el siglo xvii español.* Barcelona, 1976.
Elliott, J. H. *Imperial Spain, 1469–1716.* New York, 1969.
———. *The Revolt of the Catalans: A Study in the Decline of Spain.* Cambridge, 1963.
———. "Revolts in the Spanish Monarchy." In *Preconditions of Revolution in Early Modern Europe*, edited by Robert Forster and Jack P. Greene, pp. 109–130. Baltimore, 1970
García Martinez, Sebastià. *Els fonaments del país valencià modern.* Valencia, 1968.
Haliczer, Stephen. *The Communeros of Castile: The Forging of a Revolution, 1475–1521.* Madison, Wis., 1981.
Kamen, Henry. "The Decline of Spain: A Historical Myth." *Past and Present* 81 (November 1978):24–50.
———. "A Forgotten Insurrection of the Seventeenth Century: The Catalan Peasant Rising of 1688." *Journal of Modern History* 49 (June 1977):210–230.
———. *Spain, 1469–1714: A Society of Conflict.* New York, 1983.
———. *Spain in the Late Seventeenth Century.* New York, 1980.
Lynch, John. *Spain under the Habsburgs.* New York, 1964.
Mercader i Riba, Joan. *Felip V i Catalunya.* Barcelona, 1968.
Molas Ribalta, Pedro. *Comerç i estructura social a Catalunya i Valencia als segles xvii i xviii.* Barcelona, 1977.
Nadal, J., and Giralt, E. *La Population catalane de 1553 à 1717: L'Immigration française et les autres facteurs de son développement.* Paris, 1960.
Petrie, Charles. *The Marshal Duke of Berwick.* London, 1953.

Powell, Philip Wayne. *The Tree of Hate: Propaganda and Prejudices Affecting United States Relations with the Hispanic World*. London, 1961.
Sanabre, José. *La acción de Francia en Cataluña en la pugna por la hegemonía de Europe, 1640–1659*. Barcelona, 1976.
Scelle, George. *La traité negrière aux indes de Castille*. Paris, 1906.
Vicens Vives, Jaime. *An Economic History of Spain*. Princeton, N.J., 1969.
Vilar, Pierre. *La Catalogne dans l'Espagne moderne: Recherches sur les fondements économiques des structurales nationales*. Paris, 1962.
Voltes Bou, Pedro. *La guerra de sucesion en Valencia*. Valencia, 1964.
Walker, Geoffrey J. *Spanish Politics and Imperial Trade, 1700–1789*. Bloomington, Ind., 1979.

Index

Aigues-Mortes, 18
Albigensians, 42, 106, 107
Alicante, 91
Almanza, 100
Ampringen, Johann, 107
Anne, queen of England, 74
Arbousse, Françoise, 48
Arendt, Hannah, 4, 74
Augustus II, king of Poland, 62, 72

Barcelona, 18, 87, 89, 92, 95, 100, 101, 111
barretines, 97, 111, 112
Basville, Nicolas Lamoignon de, 2, 6, 44, 46, 51, 53
Bautista y Ramos, Juan, 25, 98
Bercsényi, Miklós, 1, 2, 25, 27, 62, 65, 71, 76, 113
Berwick, James Fitz-James, duc de, 95, 100
Besztercebánya, 71
Bethlen, Gábor, 107

Bocskai, István, 107
Boissier, Mathieu, 46
Boissonade, P., 38
Boiteuse, Marie de, 47, 48
Bonbonnoux, Jacques, 42, 46, 48, 55
Bottyán, Janos, 75
Brenner, Domokos, 74
Brès, Françoise, 21, 26, 37, 48
Brezan patent, 63
Brod, 65
Burke, Peter, 51

Cadets de la Croix, 52
Camisards blancs, 16, 52
Cantemir, Dimitrie, 61
Castanet, André, 53, 55, 56
Cavalier, Jean, 14, 25, 26, 43, 45, 47–49, 51–55, 107
Cerda, don Luis de la, duque de Medinaceli, 89
Charles I, King of Spain (Charles V, Holy Roman Emperor), 109

Charles II, King of Spain, 23, 84–86, 91, 93, 99
Charles, Archduke (later Charles VI, Holy Roman Emperor), 3, 16, 18, 25, 83, 84, 88–90, 95, 96, 98–100, 101
Charlotte Amalia von Hessen-Rheinfels, 62
Chayla, François de Langlade du, 37, 38
Churchill, John, Duke of Marlborough, 73
Cifuentes, conde de, 99
Clary, 49
Cohn, Norman, 6, 7, 17
Commissio neo acquistica, 64, 65
Copernicus, Nicholas, 12

Davies, James C., 22, 23
Debrecen, 69

Eisenstadt, S. N., 122
Elliott, J. H., 17, 110
Enriquez de Cabrera, don Juan Tomas, duque de Medina de Rioseco, 89
Érsekújvár, 71, 76
Esterhazy, Antal, 69
Esze, Tamas, 25, 62, 68, 113
Eugene of Savoy, Prince, 74

Flotard, David, 18
Forgách, Simon, 69, 70
Forster, Robert, 11
Foucault, Michel, 16
Fraissinet-de-Fourques, 53
Frangipan, Ferenc, 107

García de Avila, Francisco, 25, 98, 112
Gömör, 71
Gramsci, Antonio, 14, 15
Great Northern War, 71

Greene, Jack P., 11
Gurr, Ted, 27, 28

Hamel-Bruynincx, Jacob Jan, 73
Hegel, Georg Wilhelm Friedrich, 29
Heister, Sigbert, 2
Hesse-Darmstadt, Prince George of, 93
Hintze, Otto, xii
Hobbes, Thomas, 12
Hobsbawn, Eric, 113
Hunt, Lynn, 28

Játiva, 90, 98, 100
Johnson, Chalmers, 5, 10, 28
Joseph I, Holy Roman Emperor, 63, 71
Jung, Carl Gustav, 47
Jurieu, Pierre, 13, 45, 118

Karlowitz, Treaty of, 63
Károlyi, Sándor, 1, 75, 76
Kassa, 71
Kis, Albert, 108
Klement, Janos, 74

Lányi, Pál, 71
Laporte, Gédéon, 48
Laporte, Pierre. *See* Roland
Laqueur, Walter, 1
Le Roy Ladurie, Emmanuel, 28, 46, 48
Leopold I, Holy Roman Emperor, 10, 24, 25, 62–68, 74, 107, 114, 117
Lesczynski, Stanislaw, 61
Locke, John, 15
Lonyai, Ferenc, 71
Louis XIII, king of France, 106, 110
Louis XIV, king of France, 3, 13, 14, 18, 23, 24, 39, 42, 54, 72,

88, 92, 95, 106, 107, 111, 118, 119

Madrid, 88, 91
Mannheim, Karl, 14
Marion, Elie, 25, 43, 47–49, 55
Marlborough, John Churchill, duke of, 73
Mathieu, Marie, 48
Mazel, Abraham, 25, 37, 38, 45–47, 48, 56
Mazepa, Ivan, 61
Mohács, Battle of, 20, 108
Montrevel, Marshal, 52, 53
Moore, Barrington, 24
Mousnier, Roland, 13, 15, 16, 106
Munkács, 71

Nádasdy, Ferenc, 107
Nagyszombat, 69
Nameny Manifesto, 63
Nantes, Edict of, 13, 41–43
Niebuhr, Richard, 17
Nine Years' War, 88, 92
Noailles, Adrien Maurice, duc de, 19

Okolicsányi, Kristóf, 2
Olivares, Gaspar de Guzmán, conde-duque de, 109, 110
Ónod, Diet of (1707), 1, 2, 27, 71
Oppenheimer, Samuel, 67
Orihuela, 90

Paine, Thomas, 15
Palffy, Janos, 76
Patkul, Johann Reinhold, 61
Peras, Isabeau, 48
Perez, Antonio, 99, 109
Peter I, tsar of Russia, 72
Petrasch, Maximilian, 65
Philip II, king of Spain, 99, 110, 111

Philip IV, king of Spain, 96, 99
Philip of Anjou (later Philip V, king of Spain), 3, 9, 10, 18, 23–25, 83–85, 88–92, 94–96, 98–101, 109, 119
Pont-de-Montvert, 12
Porshnev, Boris Fedorovich, 15
Portocarrero, Luis Manuel Fernandez de (cardinal), 99
Pozsony, 69
Pozsony, Diet of, 64
Pyrenees, Treaty of, 86, 92

Rákóczi, Ferenc I, 62, 107
Rákóczi, Ferenc II, 1–3, 8, 9, 11, 16–20, 25–27, 61–63, 65, 68–72, 74–77, 107, 108, 113, 120
Rákóczi, Gyorgy I, 107
Rakovszky, Meynhert, 1, 2
Rechteren, Count Adolf Hendrik, Baron D'Almelo, 73
Rocayrol, Tobie de, 18, 55
Roland (Pierre Laporte), 5, 14, 25, 26, 48, 49, 51, 54, 55

St. John, Henry, Viscount Bolingbroke, 73
San Esteban de Gormas, conde de, 99
Saragossa, 1, 89–91, 98, 109
Sartre, Jean-Paul, 121
segadors, 108
Sequier, Esprit, 47
Seville, 87
Skocpol, Theda, 28
Soler, Antoni, 111
Spencer, Charles, earl of Sunderland, 73
Stark, Werner, 16
Stepney, George, 73
Stone, Lawrence, 5
Subtelney, Orest, 29
Surville, Isabeau, 48

Szatmár, settlement of, 73, 75–77, 108
Szécsény, 71
Szerencs, Patent of, 69

Taborites, 7
Tesse, Rene III de Froullay, comte de, 90
Thököly, Imre, 62, 67, 108
Tilly, Charles, 22, 28–30, 106, 122
Tiszáhat, 62

Utrecht, Peace of, 73

Valencia, 9, 16, 91, 98, 100, 108
Vaudois, 107
Vetes, Patent of, 69

Vienna, Treaty of, 96
Villars, Claude Louis Hector, duc de, 47, 53, 54
Villaviciosa, 96
Vincent, Isabeau, 46, 47

Waldensians, 42, 106
Werner, Ernst, 16
Wesselényi, Ferenc, 107
Wesselényi, conspiracy, 107

Zagorin, Perez, 10–12, 28
Zrínyi, Helen, 62
Zrínyi, Nicholas, 107
Zrínyi, Peter, 107

About the Authors

LINDA FREY, Professor of History at the University of Montana, and MARSHA FREY, Professor of History at Kansas State University, have worked in tandem on a number of books, including *A Question of Empire: Leopold I and the War of the Spanish Succession, 1701-1705* and *Frederick I: The Man and His Times*, and a number of journal articles. They also compiled and edited, with Joanne Schneider, the three-part bibliography *Women in Western European History* (Greenwood Press, 1982, 1984, 1986).